ARTIST POTTERS
IN ENGLAND

The Faber Monographs on Pottery and Porcelain
Former Editors: W. B. HONEY and ARTHUR LANE
Present Editors: R. J. CHARLESTON and SIR HARRY GARNER

★

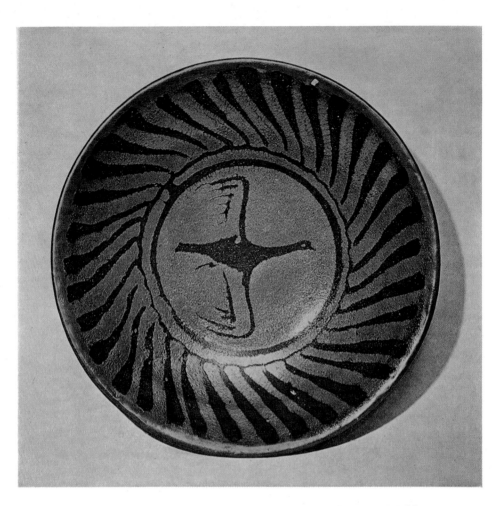

A. Stoneware Dish by Bernard Leach. 1963
Border and central decoration, 'Sea-bird
in flight', in wax-resist on *tenmoku* glaze,
with red *kaki* glaze over.
Height 2¾ inches. Width 14 inches.
In Japan.

ARTIST POTTERS
IN ENGLAND

by
MURIEL ROSE

FABER AND FABER
London

First published in 1955
by Faber and Faber Limited
24 Russell Square London W.C.1
Second edition 1970
Printed in Great Britain by
R. MacLehose and Company Limited
The University Press Glasgow
Blocks made and colour plates printed
by Fine Art Engravers Limited
Godalming
All rights reserved

ISBN O 571 04685 1

79019

FOREWORD TO THE
SECOND EDITION

Miss Rose has undertaken the difficult task of bringing up-to-date a book devoted to the work of contemporaries, and in doing so has largely re-written her original text, as well as adding a large number of fresh illustrations.

The 'sifting process' effected by time has done little to alter her original judgments, but her survey of work done since the original edition has led to an access of fresh masterpieces illustrated among the Plates. The result is an anthology of fine pots worthily commemorating the taste of an informed and sensitive observer of the modern ceramic scene.

R. J. C.

FOREWORD TO THE
FIRST EDITION

This book is the first of the series to deal at length with contemporary work. All who knew the author at the 'Little Gallery' or have followed her recent career will recognise that her long experience and knowledge, both of modern pots and potters, has enabled her to gather together in this volume a discriminating collection of the best examples in widely differing styles. It should be remembered that she has had to make her selection unaided by the sifting process that takes place with the passage of time.

Our artist potters have been criticised for the narrowness of their inspiration in adhering too closely to the finest pottery of the Far East, but the author makes it clear that, although Eastern wares provided the modern potters with their initial inspiration and are still the soundest basis for critical standards, present-day potters are increasingly influenced not only by our own traditional medieval pots but from a variety of sources.

The period is one in which developments in other arts were startling. In architecture, music and painting radically new styles appeared with growing self-consciousness and alternating optimism and despair. But in ceramic art the changes have been slower and less obvious. There has been success in pottery inspired by a rediscovery of the vitality of the arts of primitive people, but attempts to achieve originality at all costs have produced sadly disappointing results, and yet here and there, every now and then, one comes across a fine modern pot which promises the re-emergence of the elegance and vitality that mark the greatest achievements of the ceramic arts of the past.

W. B. H.

AUTHOR'S PREFACE TO
SECOND EDITION

When the first edition was prepared, fifteen years ago, artist pottery in England was only beginning its expansion and personal acquaintance with most of the best work was still feasible. Today it is no longer possible even to know all potters by name, particularly those who work in isolation or do not send their work to exhibitions. The author recognises that omissions must, therefore, be something of a certainty and offers her sincere regrets.

Thanks are again due to each one of those who have contributed to the completion of this book, particularly to those who have generously allowed their pots to be transported for illustration or supplied valuable information. Also, especially to Jane Gate, who with much patience, has provided the greater part of the new photographs and whose understanding of pots is matched by her technical skill. Once again Rosemary Edmonds and Charlotte Bawden have given their specialised help and the author also remembers with gratitude William Bowyer Honey and all he did to encourage greater understanding of the art of the potter and without whose suggestion the first edition of this book would never have been attempted.

CONTENTS

ILLUSTRATIONS

COLOUR PLATES

MONOCHROME PLATES
after page 64

11

ILLUSTRATIONS

ILLUSTRATIONS

ILLUSTRATIONS

1

THE PIONEERS:
THE FRENCH ARTIST POTTERS

In China and the Far East the art of the potter has always been held in equal honour with that of the painter or sculptor. In Europe, however, it is only in the past hundred years that serious artists have begun to consider pottery as worthy of their full attention. Prior to this the masterpieces of pottery had, with few exceptions, come to us un-named, made by craftsmen who did not think of themselves as artists and who worked almost entirely within accepted traditions.

Towards the middle of the nineteenth century a few European artists, stimulated as so often before in ceramic history by wares from the Far East, started to experiment with pottery-making. Later, after the turn of the century, the revelation of the hitherto unknown works of the early Chinese potters (brought to light when the cutting of railways disturbed the ancient tombs) aroused world-wide interest in this craft and artist potters are now at work in all parts of the world.

The enthusiasm of Paris in the middle of the last century for oriental and particularly Japanese art inspired the beginnings of present-day individual pottery-making in Europe. The pioneer French potters faced considerable difficulties. There was little exact knowledge of the chemistry of ceramics, of the relation of body to glaze or of the composition of the monochrome, *flambé* and *sang de boeuf* oriental glazes which were so much admired and which the new potters wished to rival. The classical porcelain tradition of Sèvres — the main source of technical instruction — with its rigid discipline of style imposed upon material, did not satisfy artists seeking a freer and more personal idiom born of a deeper understanding of the possibilities of their raw materials. There were few independent potters to turn to for experience. Charles Antoine AVISSEAU (1796–1861) who had set up a kiln in 1825 and Jules-Claude ZIEGLER (1804–56) an experimenter in salt-glaze, both worked in the highly individual style of Palissy, which bore little relation to the new potters' needs. There were however the French country potteries making wares for farm and household use

15

and all the more successful beginners drew upon this source of traditional skill and knowledge.

Théodore DECK (1823–91), one of the earliest of these artist potters, had the good fortune to be apprenticed at the age of nineteen to a *maître-faiencier*. He became an accomplished technician and was one of the first to realise the need for a fresh collaboration between *art et métier*. In later life he went to Sèvres and made porcelain with *flambé* glazes. His work received considerable recognition in the Paris exhibitions of Decorative Arts, which resulted in 1887 in his appointment as director of the Sèvres factory.

Auguste DELAHERCHE (1857–1940) also had his roots in a rural tradition, having attached himself at an early age to a stoneware pottery at La Chapelle-aux-Pots near his native town of Beauvais, where he made his first experiments. After an interval of ten years in Paris (during which he took over Chaplet's workshop), he returned to La Chapelle in 1894 to live the life of a recluse, firing his kiln only once a year. It is interesting to note that not until 1904 did Delaherche begin to throw his own pots and produce unique pieces, having depended hitherto, in common with other potters of the day, on the skill of a traditional thrower working to his direction and making his shapes in replica. He developed some good glazes, many of them brown of the 'tea dust' type with fine tawny markings (Pl. 2). In contrast to most of his contemporaries Delaherche gave more importance to form than to decoration.

Among these pioneers Ernest CHAPLET (1835–1909) achieved a real fusion of artist and potter. After an apprenticeship which began at the age of thirteen at Sèvres (where he studied decoration with Emile Lessore), Chaplet worked for six years in a provincial pottery at Bourg-la-Reine which made decorated earthenware. Later he abandoned the use of decoration and struggled, with inadequate knowledge, to produce glazes of the Chinese type in cuprous reds and turquoises (Pl. 1). His work shows an artist's feeling for his materials comparable to that of Delaherche, to a degree which distinguishes these two among the nineteenth-century French potters.

Jean-Charles CAZIN (1841–1901), better known as a painter, worked in stoneware, often with floral decoration (sometimes in relief) in a lively if debased Japanese style. Cazin came to England, replacing Alphonse Legros as a teacher in the Lambeth School of Decorative Art. Here and at the Fulham Pottery he met and worked with Robert Wallace MARTIN, one of the family of four brothers who since 1868 had been experimenting with individual stoneware pottery and who were using the Fulham Pottery kiln at this time. The Lambeth School of Art in South London was then a centre for the training of modellers and pottery decorators, many of whom were employed at the nearby Doulton Pottery, with which it was closely associated. At Lambeth Cazin gave instruction to young Walter MARTIN, who with his brothers may fairly claim to be the first English artist potters. Cazin returned to France about 1874, where his son Jean Michel CAZIN (1869–1917) and his daughter Berthe were both to become potters of some note.

By the turn of the century technical knowledge was accumulating and the artist potter in Paris had secured a recognised position. To this achievement Emile LENOBLE (1875–1939) (Pl. 5), stepson of Chaplet, and Emile DECOEUR (b. 1876), both working in high temperature stonewares, made the most notable contributions, carrying their experiments, particularly in the development of glazes, to a remarkable degree of control.

Emile Decoeur may be considered the most accomplished French potter of the early part of the present century. Abandoning the somewhat laboured decoration of his first period, his work shows increasingly restrained use of ornament. He commands a fine range of semi-matt glazes using white feldspar to obtain a texture resembling marble. His use of colour shows the same sensitivity, notably in bronze-blacks, a range of ochre browns (Pls. 3 and 4) and a quiet indigo-blue of great beauty. It may be this preoccupation with surface qualities which has deprived Decoeur's pots of essential vigour of form: many of them appear mechanical in shape and lack the unexpected element so vital to creative work. However it was the works of the earlier French artist potters, exhibited in the Paris exhibitions in the latter half of the nineteenth century, which stimulated the beginnings of individual pottery-making in England, since which France has played little part in its development.

In recent years, inspired largely by the work of Picasso at Vallauris, an entirely different school of potters has sprung up in France. Beyond remarking that Picasso's pottery may probably be treated more appropriately as an extension of his painting rather than as the work of an artist potter, the present monograph makes no other reference to Picasso and his followers, their pottery having as yet had little direct influence on the craft in England.

EARLY ARTIST POTTERS IN ENGLAND: THE MARTIN BROTHERS, DENISE WREN, REGINALD WELLS, THE SCHOOLS OF ART

In England the four remarkable Martin brothers were pioneers in the production of individual pottery. Their fantastic birds, jugs with winking faces, goblets, candlesticks and clock cases in brown and blue-grey salt-glaze expressed the prevailing enthusiasm for the gothic. Though it is with pottery of this kind that the Martins' name is more generally associated, their less fanciful works cannot be left out of any review of the growth of the artist potter in Great Britain.

Coming from humble origins, the Martins started with few educational advantages. Robert Wallace MARTIN (1843–1923), the eldest and always the leader, was employed early in life under Sir Charles Barry and his son as a stone carver on the new Houses of Parliament, where his taste for the grotesque was developed by a study of the fine collection of gothic casts which Pugin assembled for the inspiration of the craftsmen working on these buildings. He later made carvings for the architect J. P. Seddon, and attended the Lambeth School of Decorative Art to study modelling at the time when Jean-Charles Cazin was teaching there. At the Lambeth School Wallace also became a friend of the gifted George Tinworth and together they later studied sculpture at the Royal Academy Schools.

Lambeth had been a centre of pottery-making for at least three centuries and about the year 1862 Doulton's pottery, which made such utility wares as salt-glazed drain pipes, chimney-pots and ginger-beer bottles, began the production of decorative jugs and vases, as an addition to the traditional 'Toby' jugs with embossed figure decorations for which they had been known for a hundred years or more. In this they were encouraged by the success of the French 'Art-wares' in the Paris exhibition of 1867 and, four years later, by enthusiastic Royal patronage of Doulton products in the 1871 exhibition.[1] The

[1] For a fuller account with illustrations of Doulton's wares at this time, see Bemrose's *19th Century English Pottery and Porcelain*.

professional knowledge accumulated at Doulton's set standards in technique for the artist interested to make individual pots, but Doulton's kept their methods of colouring, decorating and particularly of salt-glaze firing a closely-guarded secret.

It was at Lambeth that Wallace Martin's deep interest in pottery was first aroused and he longed to understand the mysteries of coloured glazes and particularly the use of salt. But he also sought independence as an artist rather than attachment to Doulton's and in 1871 he left London to work for some months as modeller at a pottery near Barnstaple, probably Fishley's, where he experimented with clays. In the same year a period of employment in the Staffordshire potteries added substantially to his technical knowledge. Wallace's next move, in 1872, was to Bailey's Fulham pottery (where Dwight had produced his masterpieces in the seventeenth century). Here he again encountered Cazin and benefited from the French painter's sophisticated experience.

Walter MARTIN (1859–1912) and Edwin MARTIN (1860–1915) grew up sharing their brother's enthusiasm for pottery and in their young days both studied pottery at the Lambeth School and for a time worked at Doulton's. Being employed only as 'boys', they were not given the technical training reserved for apprentices but they took every chance of trying their hands on any wheel unoccupied by a workman. Both brothers had aspirations which could not be suppressed and had long dreamt of setting up as artist potters. In this they were encouraged by the growing public recognition of 'Artwares', following the exhibition of English pottery of this kind in South Kensington in 1871, when it was described as 'honest, useful and in thoroughly good taste' and H.M. the Queen bought a number of pieces. But it was above all the wish to understand their craft profoundly and experiment for themselves which drove them, in spite of serious lack of money, to break away from employment.

The Martin brothers first united in workshops at Pomona House near the Fulham Pottery, using that kiln from 1873–4. To secure more control over their firings and to preserve their designs and technical secrets they leased for a short time a disused glass-kiln at Shepherd's Bush. In 1877–8 they moved to Middlesex, where at Southall on the north bank of the Grand Junction Canal they built their own kiln and became independent of any industrial pottery. The kiln was a large one, firing 600 pieces. Their initial attempts at firing at the high temperature required by salt-glazing were often most painful experiments, and their output was for many years sustained at the cost of immense endurance and hardship. Wallace was the moving spirit in the team and their first pots were always signed R. W. Martin

19

scratched under the foot, together with date and place. *R. W. Martin and Bros.* or *Martin Bros. London & Southall*, with dates, appears on their later work.

Walter was the only one of the four to have trained himself on the wheel and it was he who undertook the throwing, at which he became remarkably skilful, his pots being beautifully light for their size and material. He was also the chemist and engineer and it was he who mixed the clays and was in charge of the kiln and firings, so much so that after his death the three remaining brothers found themselves seriously handicapped.

The humorous grotesques — perhaps the least acceptable of the Martin wares by present-day assessment — were largely the work of Wallace, who was the leader of the enterprise throughout. Both Wallace and Edwin were well-trained draughtsmen, as they showed in the delicacy and detail of the incised drawings decorating their wares, whether of dragons and other fantasies, or from nature as seen along the canal bank by which they worked. The shapes of Wallace's pots and his use of bands of abstract ornament could be heavy and he seems to have lacked Edwin and Walter's finer sense of the use of clay. This appears particularly in the pots made towards the end of Edwin's life, when he derived his shapes from gourds, sea-urchins and other natural objects, making gently ribbed and segmented vases which were enhanced with delicate, painstaking inlay and incised lines (Pls. 6 and 7).

Charles MARTIN (1846–1910) was the business-man and salesman. For forty years the Martins worked together producing their original wares in quantities, firing four or five times a year and occasionally making such architectural details as ornamental tiles, fireplaces or fountains.

The attempts of the nineteenth-century French potters to imitate the high-temperature Chinese glazes of the Ming and later periods were paralleled in England. Among others, Bernard Moore in Staffordshire, W. Howson Taylor in the Ruskin Pottery at Smethwick near Birmingham, and William and Joseph Burton at Pilkington's Tile-works at Clifton Junction near Manchester, all struggled to achieve richly coloured oriental glaze-effects. They aimed at quantity-production but their experiments resulted in many individual pieces. Their pots all suffer from the use of over-refined commercial bodies and glaze material, and pre-occupation with techniques suited to factory production stood in the way of creative inspiration.

In complete contrast to these is Denise WREN (b. 1891 in Albany, Western Australia), an early experimenter with an instinct for the essentials of making pottery. As a design student (1907–12) at the

Kingston-upon-Thames School of Art she came under the influence of the Manx artist Archibald Knox, a keen student of Celtic art and an inspiring teacher. Knox had designed many of the wood-block prints for silks, as well as pottery, metalwork and much else for Liberty's in their heyday. When Denise Wren began to try her hand with pottery there was neither wheel nor kiln in the Art School and she took her first pots to be fired in a flower- and chimney-pot maker's and at a church-warden pipe-maker's nearby. After watching these craftsmen at work, she persuaded the flower-pot maker to adapt an old wheel to suit her and on this she taught herself to throw. This wheel she still uses and regards as the basis of the pottery which she started in 24 Kingston Market Place in 1912. This she later transferred to Oxshott, Surrey, where in 1919, together with her husband Henry D. Wren, himself a writer and potter, they built themselves a house and pottery workshops. From her father Denise Wren had inherited a gift for invention and in 1919 she began to design and build a unique series of small high-temperature coke kilns suited to the needs of the individual potter (perhaps the first in this country), the latest of them being a salt-glaze kiln completed in 1963. No secret was made about the design of these kilns and plans of them were available to other potters at a time when such technical details were hard to discover. Denise Wren's approach has always been exploratory and romantic. She has sought variety induced by the use of relatively unrefined materials and by the action of the flame on the clay, rather than by any very calculated control (Pl. 9).

Pottery was a subject which, apart from the lustred and so-called 'Persian' wares of William de Morgan with their rich surface-decoration, had been scarcely attempted by William Morris and his workshops.

In the Art Schools teaching was, by tradition, concentrated on the Fine Arts and subjects involving design, when included in the curriculum, were described as 'Decorative' or 'Applied' Arts. As their title implies, these subjects were regarded as providing embellishment and refinement to the products of industry and belonging to an essentially different world from that of trade. The artist craftsman as we know him today hardly existed and any consideration of design as a necessary presence at every stage of manufacture had scarcely begun to be recognised. These attitudes of mind were, in part at least, a reflection of the rigid class distinctions then prevailing, in which art and the artist lived in another realm from that of the artisan and his often grimy involvement with raw materials and manual labour.

In the early years of the present century there were few publications dealing with technique which met the requirements of the

21

individual potter. For a considerable time Taxile Doat's *Les Céra-miques dl Grand Feu*, published in translation at Syracuse, New York (1903–6), was the chief source of reference. Doat, who worked at Sèvres for twenty-six years, was well known in France as an experimenter in ceramics, particularly high-temperature porcelains, and in his writings he gave drawings of kiln construction and detailed glaze recipes, mostly beyond the scope of the individual potter.

Pottery by Richard Lunn, published in 1903, was the first book of any weight to appear in England. In his introduction Lunn states that 'no previous handbooks exist suitable for use in the pottery class'. His aim was 'to help teachers and fit students for designing for the pottery industry'. The book is clearly the outcome of his gifts as a teacher and his industrial experience over a period of years as art director at the Derby Porcelain Factory. It begins with a short but comprehensive historical survey with illustrations and describes most of the essential processes including preparation of clays and glazes.

In 1914 *Pottery for Artists, Craftsmen and Teachers* by George Cox was published by Macmillan in New York and an English edition soon followed. Cox was an English artist who had worked at the Mortlake Pottery and later became an instructor at Teachers' College, Columbia University. His book is well illustrated by the author and gives kiln diagrams, descriptions of clays and their preparation and much else valuable to beginners, including his reference to the wheel as 'fountain head of all beautiful shapes'. Cox warns that scientific knowledge alone is dangerous and that formulas and analyses are of little value unless they are thoroughly understood. He also reminds his readers that the finest pottery of the past was made by men who were artists rather than chemists. In speaking of decoration Cox refers his students to Chinese and Japanese wares as sure guides and in this, as well as in his general approach to pottery making, he shows affinities with Bernard Leach.

Richard Lunn was appointed instructor in pottery at the Royal College of Art, South Kensington in 1903. In the foreword to his book, which had been published in the same year, he describes his teaching as 'the first attempt to make pottery in a school, carrying out all the processes of making, drying, firing biscuit, decorating, glazing and firing glazed ware in the class-rooms themselves'. Casting and turning are the first subjects for study in the book, and throwing is only discussed at a later stage. As elsewhere, his students followed fashion and were much occupied with painting on pottery and with the decoration of tiles in a variety of techniques. Throwing was almost entirely in the hands of a professional thrower, who attended on certain days and worked from outline drawings which students had previously prepared, many of which were also realized by casting and moulding.

22

Work at the Royal College continued on these lines and as recently as 1913 shapes were being made chiefly by slip-casting. After Lunn's death the pottery school would have closed had it not been for a small group of students, which included John Adams and Dora Billington, who had come from the Potteries and had had experience in handling clay, and these students begged to be allowed to continue, even without tuition. They were remarkably successful in teaching themselves and when a pottery department at length was re-established, it was under Dora Billington's direction.

When the Central School of Arts and Crafts was founded in London in 1894 by the incentive of W. B. Lethaby and Sydney Cockerell, pottery making was not in the syllabus and for many years the only instruction in that direction was the teaching of brush-decoration on industrially made shapes. In spite of Lethaby's influence, it was not until 1926 that pottery came to be fully taught, under the direction of Dora Billington, assisted at first, as was then generally the custom, by a traditional thrower from Doulton's.

Richard Lunn, with his industrial experience and enthusiasm for his subject, stimulated pottery teaching in schools beyond the Royal College. By 1907 he had a class at the Blackheath School of Art, chiefly for a few of the staff. Among them was George Butcher who later, as Art and Craft master at Acton County School, started probably the first attempt at pottery teaching in a secondary school.

At Camberwell School of Arts and Crafts in South London (founded 1898) pottery teaching had begun on the usual 'decorative' lines, using commercially produced glazes and bodies and employing an expert to do the throwing. Richard Lunn was brought in to teach and W. B. Dalton, Principal of the school from 1899 to 1919, became deeply interested in the subject. Mastery of the wheel and the use of materials of quality were gradually introduced and Dalton himself became an important early experimenter in stoneware in the Chinese manner.

Under Dalton's direction Camberwell provided a training ground for several potters of distinction. It was to Camberwell that Roger F R Y (1866–1934) went to continue the pottery making which he had first learnt in the autumn of 1913 from a traditional flower-pot maker in Mitcham. Inspired largely, it would seem, by the country wares of France and Italy, he confined himself to tin-glazed earthenware, undecorated and generally white, though occasionally green or blue. He sold his pots in the recently-opened Omega workshops in Bloomsbury marking them with the sign Ω in a rectangle. Fry made bowls, jugs and other useful household wares, including some handsome if unpractical large plates in both white and rich dark blue. In search of a whiter and less porous body he went to work at the Poole pottery in Dorset but the

23

outbreak of war brought Fry's experiments in pottery making largely to an end.

William Staite MURRAY, whose work belongs to a later chapter, also received some of his first instruction at Camberwell School of Art, as did Reginald WELLS (1877–1951), a sculptor who turned potter about 1909. Wells began at Coldrum near Wrotham in Kent, making earthenware with a brownish glaze, some of which he decorated with white slip in a manner recalling the Wrotham pottery of the seventeenth century. He was the first artist potter to turn to English traditions for his inspiration. Later he moved to Chelsea, and after that to Storrington in Sussex, where he set himself to make highly-fired pots in a Chinese style. Although the forms of his pots must generally be considered clumsy, he used bodies of some quality and evolved pleasant matt blue and grey-white boracic glazes, sometimes crackled, imitating Chün or Yüan (Pl. 8). He signed these with the word SOON enclosed in a rectangle.

Mention must also be made of Charles VYSE, who worked at Camberwell School of Art. He too began as a sculptor, making pottery figures. Greatly helped by his wife, an able chemist, Vyse later became interested in stoneware and produced some remarkably fine Chinese glazes with a degree of control over his medium rare at that time.

English potters of this century owe a great debt to the unusual aesthetic perception of George Eumorfopoulos. The subtle yet robust qualities of the T'ang and Sung pots, which began to come to England in numbers in the 1920's, appealed naturally to his taste and led him to purchase the nucleus of his famous collection of Chinese art. His deep understanding of early Chinese wares placed him in sympathy with contemporary potters. He made his collection available to them for study, and his attendance and purchases at exhibitions of their work not only helped them materially but did much to encourage their recognition by a wider public.

It was in the 1920's too that the Ceramic Department of the Victoria and Albert Museum, under the sympathetic keepership of Bernard Rackham, began to concern itself with contemporary artist potters. This interest, so ably developed by Rackham's successor, William Bowyer Honey, was to link the living artists with the work of the past, to the benefit of both. Appreciation of the beauties of Chinese pottery led to discovery of the qualities of our own pre-industrial wares. The sturdy English pots, with all the vitality of the soil, hitherto relegated to the departments of archaeology and folk-lore, were now recognised as works of art, to offer another and less exotic source of inspiration to the twentieth-century potter in England.[1]

[1] See Rackham's *Medieval English Pottery*.

3

BERNARD LEACH

Staite Murray, W. B. Dalton, Reginald Wells and other early twentieth-century potters who had begun to try to make high-temperature stoneware in the oriental manner in England all had to struggle with the difficulties of a technique having no traditional background. Bernard LEACH (b. 1887) was more fortunate. He was born in China (where his father was a judge) and was taken as an infant to Tokyo for upbringing by his grandparents. At the age of ten he came to school in England, to Beaumont College, and six years later entered the Slade School of Art under Tonks, as its youngest student. A short time in a bank, at his father's wish, proved unsuccessful and in 1908 Leach was studying etching under Frank Brangwyn at the London School of Art. The writings of Lafcadio Hearn aroused memories of his early childhood and in 1909, at the age of twenty-one, he decided to return to Tokyo with the intention of trying to understand the life of the East through its art. Leach took with him from England an etching-press, thinking it might appeal to the Japanese, to whom that way of making prints was then unknown, and subsequently he taught a few students. But his pupils were so skilful that he began to see himself more as a learner than a teacher. This modesty proved a talisman which endeared him to the circle of Japanese artists with whom he had begun to make friends, and disposed them to help him to an understanding of the philosophies of Far Eastern art.

Leach proceeded to build a Japanese house, married a cousin from England and put down roots. As he has told elsewhere, he was invited one day in 1911 to a party at which the guests were encouraged to decorate biscuited pots, which were then to be glazed and fired in a traditional Japanese *raku* kiln on the spot. Seeing the pots drawn red hot and transformed from the kiln excited in Leach an immediate and profound response and he decided that he must study the mysteries of this craft. Enquiry for a master led him to a humble house on the outskirts of Tokyo, to Ogata Kenzan, 'old, kindly and poor, pushed on one side by the new commercialism' but sixth in a line of master-potters stemming from the celebrated artist Kenzan I (1663–1743). There on the bare boards Leach learnt what he calls his alphabet of clay, making *raku* and stoneware pots, never supposing that eventually his master was to honour him with the *Densho*, a signed document pronouncing him, together with his friend Kenkichi Tomimoto, the only heirs to the title of Seventh Kenzan. For about a year Leach worked with Kenzan until the old man told him he was ready for more independence and, with his master's help, Leach built his first kiln in a corner of his Tokyo garden.

Meanwhile he had been finding friends among the Japanese writers and artists, the chief of these being his fellow pupil Tomimoto, architect turned potter, and Dr. Soetsu Yanagi, a philosopher whose interest in aesthetics and particularly in crafts and craftsmanship was just then beginning.

Leach began to identify himself closely with the artistic life of Japan and was the first contemporary graphic artist in that country to turn seriously to a craft. He and Yanagi together began to prepare the ground for the Japanese craft movement which was to emerge with vigour officially in 1929 and which Yanagi was to foster with much perception throughout his life. The result was a lifelong friendship, the two sharing a belief in the value of the crafts not only as a means of artistic expression but as an antidote to the materialism of mass-production and a way of livelihood satisfying to the whole man.

Leach has called Japan 'a paradise for potters' with its established traditional skills and accessible raw materials. Japan, too, enjoyed a tradition of subtle critical appreciation of craftsmen's pots handed down by the Tea-masters, criteria which the Western potter sadly lacks. Also, ceramic masterpieces from China, Korea and Japan could be studied in public and private collections — particularly early pots of a style and quality at that time unknown in Europe.

By now pottery was clearly Leach's vocation. He travelled about Japan seeing fine pots and visiting country potters, and working in their kilns. But he felt the need to study Far Eastern art at its sources and spent the years 1916–18 in Pekin and also went to Korea. Leach returned to Japan in 1919 and bought and rebuilt old Kenzan's stoneware kiln on a new site outside Tokyo. There he first met Shoji Hamada (b. 1892) who had just left the Institute of Pottery in Kyoto and had been inspired by the work of Leach and Tomimoto to devote himself to hand-made pottery.

Leach had been absorbing Far Eastern aesthetics and techniques now for eleven years and he was feeling the need to return home and test his acquired skills in his native land, and in 1920 he returned with his family to England accompanied by Shoji Hamada. At the suggestion of Mrs. Frances Horne, and with her support, Leach chose for his pottery a site with a small stream on high ground about a mile outside St. Ives in Cornwall. Here with Hamada's invaluable collaboration he began building a small two-chambered climbing kiln of Japanese style and providing modest working accommodation.

Their first months were largely spent in looking, in a virtually treeless land, for wood for firing the kiln, and for clay and other pottery materials. The preparation of both clays and glazes from natural sources by simple methods which retained inherent qualities and characteristic impurities had been a basic part of Leach's experience in Japan and was an aspect of pottery technique quite unrealized in England at that time. Leach was fortunate in finding in Cornwall many valuable sources of supply for his work. Together he and Hamada, carrying binoculars, surveyed the neighbourhood on foot. From an inland hill top they saw a red cleft in the granitic landscape which led them to St. Erth railway station, where nearby they found a pit with red plastic clay (used by the tin miners to hold the candles in their helmets) and fine water-worn sand. Other materials were near at hand. China clay from St. Austell, unique in its freedom from the tinges of iron, and feldspar and Cornish stone to grind for glazing. Ingredients for vegetable-ash glazes came from the burning of threshing chaff or of reeds from the St. Erth valley and from hardwood sawdust, as well as direct from the kippering industry in St. Ives.

Lake's pottery in Truro, not far from St. Ives, was still making red earthenware Cornish pitchers in quantity for local domestic use, as well as other household wares. In such surviving rural potteries and in local museums Leach with Hamada at hand studied his native traditions and fused them with the knowledge he had already gained in the East. In the lively decorated dishes of Toft and in later slip-wares and above all in the noble forms of English medieval pottery Leach recognised many qualities he had learned to value in Japan. As a potter he saw in the vigorous handles of medieval jugs, and the integral part they played in the form of the whole pot, principles which he could put to practical use (Pls. 12 and 25). This conception, together with slipwear techniques, he was later to transmit to Japan, a country without a tradition for handles as we know them.

In St. Ives Leach had begun by making the *raku* (Pls. 10 and 11) and stoneware he had studied in the East but very early he was including slip-decorated lead-glazed earthenware in the English manner (Pls. 14 and 15). Combed and trailed slipwares, especially moulded dishes, inspired him to attempt some twentieth-century counterparts. The tradition of combing had been almost lost, and it was only after long experiment that Leach and Hamada, together with Michael Cardew, discovered that the combed decoration made by mingling wet slips of contrasting colours, must be poured and trailed on to the flat clay and the whole

27

dried to leather hardness before being placed over a biscuited mould (Pls. 16 and 17). This method of shaping dishes, and the whole technique of trailed slip, Hamada took back to Japan, where it has now been adopted by several country potteries — one of the rare instances of an English contribution to oriental ceramic skills.

At this time the St. Ives kilns were fired with wood, coal being used only for starting. Leach's method of firing was an essential part of his philosophy and technique: his work gained much of its quality from the direct contact of the flames with the pots (where these were not in saggars), the fragments of falling wood-ash and the variations caused by the alternate oxidation and reduction natural with a wood-stoked fire. This practice had necessarily somewhat uncertain and occasionally disastrous results but these were accepted as part of the price to be paid for quality in the successful pots. Leach used his large kiln chiefly for his stoneware but had a traditional Japanese up-draught kiln for the lower temperature wares, *raku*, slipware and biscuit. This too was wood-fired and was constructed so that the long flames from resinous wood could play on the shelves or through perforated saggars on to the glazed ware — the manner of firing similar to that which had produced the English pre-industrial earthenwares with their variety and warmth of colour not to be gained in more sophisticated types of kiln.

Leach always considered the discipline of making pots that fulfil the exacting conditions of comfortable daily use in the kitchen and on the table (Pl. 21) to be of equal importance with the consideration he gave to his individual pieces and a valuable complement to them. It was for practical reasons therefore that he abandoned the making of the porous fragile *raku*-glazed wares, which had proved unsuitable for English use.

In 1922 Tsurunoske Matsubayashi, engineer, chemist and hereditary craftsman potter—the 39th generation of a well-known Kyoto family of potters—arrived from Japan. He came to help Leach and Hamada and designed and worked on the building of a three-chambered traditional Japanese down-draught climbing kiln which, with modifications, is still in use in St. Ives. By 1923, when Hamada returned to Japan, Leach was beginning to attract a few student apprentices — notably Michael Cardew and Katherine Pleydell Bouverie. Matsubayashi brought timely knowledge, not only of kiln construction but also of clay plasticity and the chemistry of pottery in general. He remained in St. Ives until after the first firing of the new kiln in 1924.

Leach's work had found a ready sale in Japan but circumstances in England were by no means so favourable. Though his pots attracted enthusiastic notice from a discriminating few, they barely allowed

B. STONEWARE BOTTLE BY BERNARD LEACH. 1952
Decoration painted, incised and impressed.
Height 16¼ inches. Marks: BL & St. Ives seals.
Bendicks (Mayfair) Ltd.

him a living: the public interested in buying hand-potters' work was still a small one and was further diminished by the industrial depression of the late 1920's. In these experimental years the pottery could scarcely have maintained itself without help. Kiln losses were as high as 20%, and not more than 10% of pots were up to show standards. Leach was exhausting his capital, and Mrs. Horne's St. Ives Handicraft Guild, which had sponsored his arrival in St. Ives, had come to an end. It was friends in Japan who, by arranging exhibitions of pots and drawings and sending him all the proceeds, enabled Leach to establish his pottery in his own country. In England sales of pots were for the most part direct from St. Ives, with exhibitions in London, particularly at Paterson's Gallery in Bond Street, which was making a reputation for shows of artist potters' work. Leach, Hamada and William Staite Murray all held exhibitions of their work at Paterson's Gallery and for the first time pottery began to receive the serious attention of art critics, foremost among whom was Charles Marriott, whose notices in *The Times* were written with unusual understanding, not only of the potter's achievements but also with knowledge of his technical problems, a service regrettably absent today. Stoneware tiles, plain and decorated, were developed from 1930 onwards, and about this time Leach's eldest son David decided to join his father's workshop.

In 1933 Bernard Leach left St. Ives for a while and, with the help of Leonard and Dorothy Elmhirst, built a small pottery at Shinner's Bridge near Dartington Hall in South Devon. Here, in a Japanese updraught kiln, he developed his slipware techniques, hardening the body by higher firing (up to 1,200°C) thus making the wares more durable, and achieving some particularly fine combed slipware dishes. A year later, accompanied by Mark Tobey, the American artist, Leach went back to the Far East for a period of work with Hamada, to travel in Japan and Korea, and to take stock of the growing craft movement in these countries.

On returning to England in 1936, generously encouraged by the Elmhirsts, Leach began to write a practical guide for the artist potter. In *A Potter's Book*, which was published in 1940, he set down without reserve all his accumulated experience, both technical and aesthetic. In the preparation of this book Leach submitted his MS to his friend Henry Bergen, a New England scholar of Middle English who had settled in London and who haunted the potters from their earliest showings. Bergen was able to offer valuable comment for he had an unusual and appreciative knowledge of Japanese pottery, as well as a critical and very precise mind. *A Potter's Book* has been reprinted many times and become a working handbook for potters throughout the world. Although its first concern is with the potter's practical problems, Leach writes always as an artist and never overlooks the importance of those qualities which can make even the simplest pot something more than merely useful.

The development of artist-made pottery in the first half of the twentieth century owes quite as much to Leach's writing and teaching as to his work as a potter. These have tended to divide his energies with the result that his pots have at times been uneven in quality. But in recent years, particularly since 1955, the output of fine pots has been steadily maintained, confirming all the promise of the earlier work.

Leach's pots always have a sensitive glaze-body relationship, well considered at the outset, a virtue often overlooked by other potters. His best shapes are lively and the sense of conception of the pot in the round is always evident, although he works largely from a number of quick sketches of ideas for pots from which he later chooses those he wishes to develop. But it is in decoration that Leach excels, not only because he has the command of hand of an accomplished draughtsman but also because he has an instinct for the right placing of decoration and for economy in its use, to both of which he has given much thought. He follows the oriental practice of repeating a decorative idea on different pots over a long period of time, during which it develops, apparently unconsciously. The bird's nest shown in its recent form in Plate 20 had appeared twenty-five years earlier in trailed slip on large earthenware plates, and its progressive variations, particularly in the treatment of the birds' heads, illustrates Leach's capacity for change and development, and his instinctive response to the underlying currents of artistic thought. (See also Pls. 13 and 16).

Leach sometimes uses modelled animal-forms for knobs or handles. He commands a far wider range of techniques of decoration than any of his contemporaries, including brushwork, wax resist, inlay, *sgraffito*, stamping, paper stencils and combed and trailed slip and in Japan he has very successfully employed over-glaze enamels (Pl.22a). In collaboration with his son David the making of hand porcelain (Pl. 23b) and porcellaneous stoneware was developed at St. Ives, which later provided the basis for the work of Harry Davis and other potters.

Bernard Leach, and with him Hamada, changed the English artist potter's whole approach to his craft. They brought a conception of the pot as a whole which included thoughtful treatment of the foot (and any marks it might carry) and realization of the inseparable relation of body to glaze. By stressing the importance of the intimate understanding of raw materials which follows the preparation of bodies and glazes by the potter himself, they revealed a subtle medium of expression of which Western artists had hitherto been largely ignorant.

30

C. STONEWARE BOTTLE BY SHOJI HAMADA. 1935
Tenmoku glaze with wax-reserve brush decoration.
Height 14 inches. No Mark.
Walker Art Gallery, Liverpool.

4

SHOJI HAMADA, MICHAEL CARDEW, KATHERINE PLEYDELL BOUVERIE AND NORAH BRADEN

Although most of his working life has been in Japan, Shoji HAMADA (b. 1892) commands attention in any consideration of artist potters in England in the first half of this century. His earliest exhibitions in London, while he was first working with Leach and still to some extent feeling his way, at once excited the English potters (Pl. 28). As much by the impact of his personality as by his work he may be said to have had an influence equal to that of Leach and much more far reaching than Staite Murray's.

Coming of Japanese country stock, Hamada brings to his work a breadth and vigour which immediately distinguish it. His early studies at the Institute of Pottery in Kyoto included scientific experiments into the composition of the glazes of early Chinese pottery, and when, later, he had gained a mastery of his technique he appeared, in the manner of all good artists, to have forgotten it. He works almost entirely in stoneware and shows many of the qualities which the self-conscious artist of today finds hardest to release. His pots combine to an unusual degree rough, apparent casualness with extreme subtlety both in form and colour. His brushwork can rise to a lyric sensibility (Pls. 30 and 33) and has a notable strength and freedom — the heritage from generations for whom the brush has been the accepted tool for writing and drawing.

Hamada came to England with Leach in 1920 to learn by experience in establishing a new pottery on untried ground. His value to Leach, and to the early students at the Leach pottery, was in no small part due to the humility with which he approached his work. The results of early St. Ives firings were fairly unpredictable, and in disgust Hamada would throw many of his own pots, as they came from the kiln, into the nearby stream, from which others would later retrieve them. Before long he gave up marking his work with any personal seal, and when he returned to Japan in 1923 he preferred to join the unique country-

31

pottery community in Okinawa where, as he has written, 'I had nothing to give, I had only to learn and to follow', rather than accept the official position offered to him. Later he chose to live and work in Mashiko, a village of potters eighty miles north of Tokyo which supplies the bulk of the domestic and kitchen pots for that city. In Mashiko he decided to learn to master the somewhat difficult local clay instead of bringing in better clay from elsewhere, a process which he admits took him 20 years. It was not until about eight years after his return to Japan, and another short period of work in England in 1929–30 (Pls. 29, 30 and 31), that he built his own kiln, having until then used the communal kilns of Mashiko.

Hamada has continued to send his work to London, where its mature qualities receive increasing recognition. In 1952 he came again to England and held an exhibition in London which showed the mastery with which he is able to use what appear to be casual accidents of technique as part of the design of the pot as a whole, thus bringing to the work both the charm of surprise and a sense of easy command of his medium. In recent years his use of slab-built and moulded pots (Pls. 38 and 39) has influenced the younger potters, and the effect of Hamada's very personal style is evident in other ways, as for instance in the use of poured decoration.

Leach has described Hamada as 'well ballasted'. To see him at work, particularly at the wheel, is unforgettable and impresses the layman almost as deeply as it does the potter. Probably this comes from his complete unselfconsciousness and striking absence of any tension whilst in such evident command of his ideas and material.

Of the English potters, Michael CARDEW (b. 1901) comes nearest to Hamada's breadth of approach and natural feeling for clay. Cardew's interest in pottery began in childhood. His home was full of handmade pots and each summer he was taken by his father to visit the country pottery at Fremington, near Barnstaple, where they were made. This pottery was then in the hands of Edwin Beer Fishley, a traditional potter of distinction making North Devon pitchers and other brown and green galena-glazed earthenware, including domestic wares as well as more 'artistic' products. Fishley died in 1911 and it was from his grandson, W. Fishley Holland, at Braunton, in North Devon, that in 1921 Cardew learnt to throw, while still an undergraduate at Oxford. Turning to pottery-making in reaction from the intellectual world of the classical scholar, he resolved upon a serious study of pottery, and with this urge to make rather than to reason went back to Braunton. But the Braunton pottery, removed from the old pottery at Fremington which had been in the Fishley family since the early nineteenth century, did not hold Cardew for long.

D. SLIPWARE JUG BY MICHAEL CARDEW. 1928-30
Height 9½ inches. Mark: Winchcombe pottery seal.
Charlotte Bawden.

He was seeking wider experience when a short article on Bernard Leach in the *Pottery Gazette* aroused his curiosity. A visit in July 1923 to Lake's traditional pottery in Truro led on to St. Ives, and in the following November Cardew joined Leach as the first of his pupils. Cardew brought with him news of the North Devon earthenware tradition with its bowed and pulled handles, and a Devon kickwheel, where hitherto only a Japanese stick-propelled wheel had been used. His wish was to rediscover all he could of the English slipware tradition and at this time stoneware did not hold the same interest for him. Cardew learnt much from Leach, above all the importance of form, the need to aim at the completeness so strongly realized in our traditional wares, 'like a full moon' as Leach put it, and capable of being at its finest in the most primitive pots.

In June 1926 Cardew rented a country pottery at Winchcombe in Gloucestershire, which had previously produced red flower-pots and large domestic pans but had been closed since 1915. One of the former workers, Elijah Comfort, was willing to return and Cardew was fortunate in having the benefit of his experience and skill. The Winchcombe pottery had a large bottle-shaped up-draught kiln, entered on two levels and fired with coal and wood, and a hovel or upper chamber in the base of the chimney for biscuit firing. This kiln could hold up to three thousand pieces and when Cardew became established firing normally took place every two or three months. (Both kiln and pottery are well described with drawings in Thomas Hennell's *The Countryman at Work*, published in 1947.)

Cardew's first years at Winchcombe were spent in learning to fire the great kiln and in overcoming difficulties with materials, and it was not until about 1928 that he began to produce good pots. He started by using red Devon clay from Fremington, then experimented unsuccessfully with clay from a local brickyard which proved full of iron, and finally began to dig in a field adjoining the pottery. With a horse to work the pug-mill he washed and pugged this clay himself.

Cardew set to work to produce household earthenware pots in quantity, lead-glazed and decorated with trailed or combed slip, or with a pattern scratched through both glaze and slip, in the spirit of earlier English slipware (Pls. 40 and 41). Jugs, bowls, casseroles, teapots, baking dishes and many other useful shapes were turned out in abundance. He also made a number of large jars fitted with wooden spigots, for the storage of draught beer, home-brewed wine or cider, of which two examples are shown in Plates 43 and 47. After some years of struggle his work — produced in repetition and therefore not expensive — found a reasonably steady market, a good deal of it being bought locally. It has been said that Cardew should not be assessed on solitary examples of his work: only the sight of the storage loft at Winchcombe after a firing, the wide floor covered with stacks of golden-brown dishes, jugs, mugs, cider jars and much else, could give a full idea of the range and force of his ability.

Cardew's early work, much of it light in colour, of which the best collection is that purchased by Sydney Greenslade for the University College of Wales in Aberystwyth, shows especially the rich variations resulting from his method of wood-firing. Later he more frequently used black slip, often decorated with trailed white slip, and sometimes in his last years at Winchcombe he introduced copper green. His first important exhibition was in 1931 in the Royal Institute Galleries, and he reached the peak of his development in earthenware about the year 1938, when he held a memorable exhibition at the Brygos Gallery in London and showed, together with many other fine pots, three large bowls about fifteen inches in diameter. The best of these bowls, perhaps the most exciting piece of slipware made in England since the eighteenth century, was bequeathed by Henry Bergen to the Hanley Museum and is shown in Plate 45, though reproduction does not convey its scale, range of colour and breadth of feeling.

Cardew is rarely successful with pots which are not designed for a particular purpose and has never attempted to make purely decorative pieces. He is always at his best when throwing on a large scale where his natural strength of form can show itself, and his work at Winchcombe has to a remarkable degree the unpretentious directness of English pre-industrial country pottery.

Of Cornish origin, Cardew had studied the Cornish language and traditions, and had always wished to return to his native county. In 1939 he left the Winchcombe pottery in the hands of Raymond Finch, who had joined him as apprentice about three years earlier, and settled at Wenford Bridge near Bodmin in Cornwall. Here he built a new kiln and began to try changes in technique. He experimented for a time with tin-glazed earthenware but felt more and more drawn to the making of stoneware. War and a return for a period of work at Winchcombe interrupted his experiments and in 1942 he accepted the post of pottery-instructor at Achimota College in the Gold Coast (now Ghana), where as teacher he followed Kenneth Murray and Harry Davis, both former St. Ives pupils. However, the closing of the pottery school three years later brought his work in the College to an end. Accepting a grant of money in lieu of a return passage to England, with a few of his African students Cardew moved to Vumé-Dugamé on the Volta River, seventy miles from Accra, a village making large unglazed red earthenware pots but where the potter's wheel and kiln were then unknown. Here he constructed a pottery and began the production of stoneware, using only the resources of the immediate neighbourhood both in the making of his kiln, wheel and other equipment and for his raw materials. The village clay provided his bodies, he obtained his glazes by mixing wood-ash with finely ground local feldspar, clay and oyster-shell, and also found a source of natural iron oxide which could be used to lively effect in brush decoration. At Vumé Cardew produced a unique group of pots, most of them having rich bronze-green or bluish ash-glazes in which the iron decoration often flashes a brilliant rusty orange. The finest of these is the jar illustrated in Plate 50, the form of which, particularly in the lip, derives from the local waterpots and which in colour and decoration (drawn from the Vumé lily) breathes its tropical origin. Cardew did not go to Vumé with any intention of teaching the local potters. If they cared to benefit by his greater technical knowledge and experience, then his work and his equipment were there for them to see.

Returning to Wenford Bridge in 1948, he began to reorganise the pottery and rebuild his kiln for the making of stoneware, which now so absorbed him that any work at a lower temperature was not to be thought of. The problems he had had to meet both in West Africa and at Wenford, particularly the higher temperatures he was now using, led him to an increasingly scientific approach to his work, in contrast to his Winchcombe period, when he had dismissed scientific knowledge as better ignored. He remained at Wenford Bridge long enough to produce some pots of distinctive character, mostly light cream (Pl. 49) or pale blue-grey in glaze, with brush decoration. But he could not forget West Africa and in 1950 accepted an appointment as Pottery Officer to the Commerce and Industries Department of the Nigerian Government.

On arrival in Nigeria Cardew travelled about the country observing its traditions and resources. In 1951 he set up a Pottery Training Centre at Abuja in Northern Nigeria and began to introduce wheel-thrown stoneware. The local low-temperature pottery, though well suited to primitive methods of cooking and living, was just beginning to be found unsuitable. Tables, plates and more sophisticated methods of cooking and eating were coming into use, as well as the drinking of tea and coffee, and the stronger stoneware met a variety of needs (Pls. 51–53). Cardew's aim was never to 'improve' the local pottery, which was perfectly suited to its previous uses, but to put the craftsmen in the way of meeting changing manners of life.

Michael Cardew's term of employment by the Nigerian Government came to an end in 1965 and he returned to Cornwall, to his pottery at Wenford Bridge. There he has installed labour-saving machinery and is establishing a teaching workshop where he plans to have Africans among his students.

During his stay in Nigeria Cardew had begun a close study of geology, a knowledge of which he considers very necessary to the potter. From time to time he has held courses on the subject in Wenford during which visits are made to local areas of geological value to potters. This is an unforgettable experience for those who have attended, if only for the way in which Cardew can hold his audience spellbound while he talks passionately about a little earth lying in the palm of his hand.

When Michael Cardew moved from the Winchcombe pottery to work in Cornwall he did not give up his interest there. He had left it in the care of Raymond FINCH (b. 1914), who had come to him in 1936 after two terms at the Central School of Arts and Crafts in London. Cardew returned once for a brief spell of work in Winchcombe but Finch never left it and eventually bought the pottery in 1946 (Pl. 70). Throughout much of its life the Winchcombe pottery has had the support of Sydney Tustin, Cardew's first pottery boy, who developed into one of the finest throwers in the country. His jugs in particular have a lightness and balance of form which distinguish them. Slowly the great kiln became too old for work and in 1960 Finch changed his production to stoneware. He makes only domestic pots, amongst the best of which are his casseroles, (Pl. 71), and in recent years has been exporting bulk orders to Scandinavia.

Katherine PLEYDELL BOUVERIE (b. 1895) had her compelling first sight of stoneware at an early Leach exhibition in 1923. Her request to become a student at St. Ives did not immediately succeed and she studied for a short time at the Central School of Arts and Crafts, where Dora Billington was teaching pottery. But in 1924 she joined Leach's pottery at the moment when Hamada and Matsubayashi, an experienced potter from Japan, were both there. Cardew had recently arrived and Norah Braden was shortly to follow. Although Matsubayashi was chiefly concerned with building a larger kiln, from time to time in the evenings he gave instruction in pottery technology, discoursing on clay plasticity, the chemistry of glazes and pottery in general and, of course, on kiln construction. At such times Katherine Pleydell Bouverie took careful notes which were to stand her in good stead. In 1925 she left St. Ives, inviting Matsubayashi to help her in the construction of a wood-fired stoneware kiln adjoining the water-mill at Coleshill in Wiltshire. Here Norah BRADEN (b. 1901) joined her in 1928 and they worked together for eight years. The variety of timber and other vegetation on the Coleshill estate enabled Katherine Pleydell Bouverie to carry out a series of experiments with glazes obtained from wood and plant

ashes, research which had not previously been attempted systema-
tically in England. Many of these glazes were of excellent surface
texture and colour, creamy matt-whites and light greys derived
from grass or reed-ash, enhanced sometimes by a defined crackle;
bronzy olive greens, dark browns and lighter greens from the ash of
various trees; and a particularly beautiful quiet blue from the ash of
laurustinus. These glazes were all made after the same formula: a
measured quantity of ash, previously prepared by burning on a clean
hearth, then washed and finely sieved, plus the same part of feldspar, was added to a half-part of ball clay from Dorset (Pls. 55a and b).

To vary their output of glazed pots Katherine Pleydell Bouverie
and Norah Braden, who did not make table wares, produced unglazed
pots and bowls (in graduated sizes) with drainage for growing plants.
For these they used a carefully prepared light-coloured body of fairly
coarse texture which fired pale-grey to white, or creamy pink when in
an oxidizing atmosphere.

Norah Braden arrived at St. Ives after three years mainly spent
studying drawing in the Royal College of Art. Leach considered her
in many ways his most gifted pupil. Her output was always small and
she destroyed much of it but what remains shows proof of unusual
talent. Examples of her pots are in the Victoria and Albert Museum,
notably a stoneware bowl (Plate 56) in which the subtlety of detail
and fine glaze can only be fully appreciated when the bowl is handled.
She is an artist of sensitive ability, a fine draughtsman and possessed of
incisive powers of criticism, and it is much to be regretted that she
virtually ceased working as a potter when she left Coleshill in 1936.

Katherine Pleydell Bouverie continued alone until war interrupted
her work in 1940. In 1946 she moved to Kilmington Manor in
Wiltshire, where she built an oil-fired kiln. In contrast to Norah
Braden, who sometimes used brush decoration, Katherine Pleydell
Bouverie's pots depend largely on the quality and variety of their
glazes, which she sometimes emphasizes by slight angularities of form,
in ribbing or lobed panels (Plate 54). She has been a valuable consultant to many of the younger potters, always most generous with her
knowledge, particularly in the matter of glazes.

5

THE LEACH POTTERY:
DAVID LEACH, KENNETH QUICK,
WILLIAM MARSHALL,
RICHARD BATTERHAM

In establishing his pottery at St. Ives Bernard Leach never thought of it as the studio of a secluded artist. It was always his intention that it should become, as it did, a place for the exchange of pottery knowledge and for work by a group of craftsmen in conditions that were mutually congenial. He believed in the value to the artist potter of producing pots for daily household use, in addition to individual more highly priced pieces. Leach also sought to make the former at a price which would bring them within the means of all who might wish to buy them. This called for repetition without the loss of quality and for organised planning of the whole pottery.

From the outset Bernard Leach's generous personality and first-hand knowledge of oriental techniques attracted students to St. Ives. Here there were no technical mysteries, secret glaze recipes and the like — all information was pooled and freely shared. Experience in throwing came largely from the making of useful wares in repetition, and from the early days of the pottery student apprentices provided much of the labour. For many years the only permanent paid hand at the St. Ives pottery was George Dunn, who had attached himself to the pottery literally from its first days. Dunn was a racy Cornish character, never at a loss either with the summer visitor or the new student. He came of a St. Ives fishing family and after many adventurous years at sea, spent the rest of his life at the pottery, where he was succeeded by Horatio Nelson Dunn, one of his twenty-three children.

Michael CARDEW, later to become the most distinguished of Leach's pupils, went to St. Ives in 1923 determined to make English slipware, and his vitality gave much of the incentive to Leach's early work in this direction. At this period Katherine Pleydell Bouverie, and later Norah Braden and Charlotte Epton, were among the team of talented students who were attracted to the workshop. A summer course for a small group of students and teachers of pottery, generally not more than six, was held annually and benefited many beginners.

When David LEACH (b. 1910) decided to follow his father, his apprenticeship in pottery naturally began at St. Ives. In search of more exact understanding and control of his materials, and to complement his father's largely empirical approach, he spent a year at the Stoke-on-Trent College of Technology. On his return he was able to test his new knowledge in workshop practice, and carry through some valuable reorganization and also take charge of the pottery during his father's absences in Japan and elsewhere. The demand for the useful wares was rising and it was clear that a more stable control of output was necessary if the flow was to be maintained. In 1937 it was decided to convert the three-chambered climbing kiln (under David's direction) for firing with oil and electric air blower, and electric test kilns were also installed which enabled a series of glaze and body tests to be carried out. It was also agreed to abandon the making of slipware, replacing it with the more durable and versatile stoneware, and the workshop settled down to a steady output, chiefly of domestic pots, which before long justified the production of a small illustrated catalogue. The prototypes were Leach's designs, and standards, particularly in throwing, were upheld by mutual criticism and the master's watchful eye. A basic craft cannot be learnt quickly by intensive study. The knowledge must grow out of practical experience with the hands over a considerable period of time until the nature and right usage of materials becomes instinctive. A skill, such as the rhythmic kneading of clay or the use of the wheel, has to be mastered by repetition until it is virtually subconscious. The eyes also have to learn to see with critical perception.

The numbers working in the St. Ives pottery are kept to a total of not more than twelve since Leach believes this to be about the maximum number who can keep in touch with every aspect of the work and combine together. Glazes are in a limited range, chiefly celadon, *tenmoku* black, *kaki* iron red and a creamy oatmeal which lends itself to decoration in olive and quiet blue.

Among the students who worked at St. Ives in the 1930's and who subsequently became established potters were Harry and May DAVIS, who in 1946 set up the Crowan Pottery, converting a water-mill at Praze in Cornwall with great ingenuity, using the water power to help in the production of very efficient, moderately priced stoneware for the table. In 1962 they emigrated, with much of their equipment, to New Zealand, where there is an active interest in hand-made pottery and where they are again in full production.

39

In 1938 St. Ives began the experiment of engaging local untrained lads as apprentices in order to ensure continuity of labour against the changing flow of students, whose conditions of engagement required a stay of two years. All who work in the pottery have opportunities to make some pots of their own, and Kenneth QUICK (1931–63), a St. Ives boy who joined the pottery in 1945, had genuine natural gifts (Plate73). Unhappily these were never fully realised since he was drowned while bathing during a visit to Japan. The first of these apprentices was William MARSHALL (b. 1923), who became a skilled thrower and through the years has matured into a potter in his own right. He remains at St. Ives as senior craftsman and has had exhibitions in London and elsewhere. His work is uneven in quality but at his best he succeeds in using the familiar pottery materials and techniques with a freshness which is successfully his own (Plate 75).

So many students have taken and given at St. Ives that it is impossible to mention more than a very few. Warren and Alix MACKENZIE, two American potters with considerable previous experience, joined Leach in 1950, returning to Minneapolis in 1952, where Warren Mackenzie is now instructor in pottery in the University of Minnesota

In 1955 David LEACH and his brother Michael, who had worked in his father's pottery for five years, both decided to set up their own workshops — the latter at Fremington in North Devon. David settled at Bovey Tracey in South Devon and divides his time between teaching and making pots. In a very successful exhibition at the Craftsmen Potters' Association in 1966, the full range of his work could be seen. He is generous in sharing his knowledge with other potters who consult him not only over technical problems but also for his experience in the planning and management of a small pottery (Pl. 72).

Among the younger students the work of Richard BATTERHAM (b. 1936) claims attention. From boyhood Batterham had thought of being a potter and Bryanston, where he went to school, decided the issue. The school pottery was under the enthusiastic and very able guidance of Donald Potter and such boys as wished could spend much of their free time practising on the wheel or mastering the use of the large wood-fired kiln and learning, at a professional standard, about pottery-making generally. On leaving school Batterham went to work in the Leach pottery for two years, at a time when, fortunately for both of them, Hamada's son Atusya was also one of the apprentices. Batterham has always known where he was going and by the time he left St. Ives he had planned his future in some detail. He bought a cottage in Durweston, near Blandford, Dorset, with enough space to enable him to start potting, and began to produce well designed, soundly made domestic stoneware. After six years of work in rather cramped quarters he completed the building of a pottery close to his home, the planning of which is the result of his realistic experience. He employs no assistant or apprentice and has only lately started to extend his range, which he does not mark, and to try his hand at making other than strictly useful pots, a beginning which holds definite promise (Pls. 76 and 77).

6

WILLIAM STAITE MURRAY, THOMAS SAMUEL HAILE, HENRY FAUCHON HAMMOND, PAUL BARRON

The development of William STAITE MURRAY (1881–1962) as a potter was quite independent of what was happening in St. Ives. After early work in engineering, and practice as a painter both in England and abroad, he began, about the year 1912, to experiment with pottery in Kensington, making low-temperature wares with brush decoration in colour, using a gas-fired kiln. Demobilised at the end of the First World War, he embarked on stoneware in a pottery which he set up in his brother's engineering works in Rotherhithe. At this period his pots generally followed prevailing clichés, concentrating on glaze effects on a flinty commercial body, splashed or streaked but otherwise without decoration, on high-shouldered shapes with indeterminate openings: on these, after the usual custom, he scratched his name, William S. Murray or W. S. Murray, under the foot of the pots, sometimes adding date and place. From an early stage Staite Murray was concerned with the science of his craft. He made many experiments, particularly in modifications to kiln design, to gain greater control over his results. Leaving Rotherhithe, he built at Brockley in Kent a two-chambered kiln for high-temperature wares, claimed to be the first crude-oil-burning kiln for the individual potter in England, an invention which he patented. Although Murray had earlier attended the Camberwell School of Art, he acquired his accomplished technique largely through persistent personal experiment.

In the early 1920's, after Murray had seen an exhibition of Hamada's pots, and as a result of talks with him, a complete change came over his work. His bodies, formerly white and characterless, were now invigorated by a sandy texture, often firing an ochre yellow or light red. His glazes no longer entirely covered his pots, and brushwork (Pl. 61) or scratched decoration sometimes appeared. His forms became inventive to the point of exaggeration, and soon after this alteration in style he began to sign his work with an impressed seal, M in a pentagon.

Murray's pottery soon claimed attention and was exhibited alongside paintings by some of the livelier of the young artists of the day, Ben Nicholson, Christopher Wood and others. This was significant, for Murray aspired to gain acceptance for pottery as a medium comparable to painting or sculpture — as a form, in fact, of abstract art, which was then being so much discussed. The making of useful wares never interested him and all his later one-man shows were held at the Lefèvre Galleries, an established centre for painting exhibitions of the best repute. He gave each pot a title and placed what were then thought to be very high prices on his work, and his attitude in general probably increased the prestige of the individual potter.

In 1925 Murray was appointed head of the Pottery School in the Royal College of Art at South Kensington, where many students passed through his classes, though it was only to a chosen few that he gave his full attention and on the most gifted of these he made a lasting impression.

After his meeting with Hamada, Staite Murray's work grew increasingly personal, both in form and decoration, although some of his shapes and the thumb-marked feet which he adopted about 1936 show the influence of English medieval earthenware. The feet of most of Murray's later pots are conspicuous, sometimes even obtrusive, a characteristic which he passed on to more than one of his pupils. In spite of a deadness of form due to extensive turning in some of the large pieces, his work gives evidence of powerful ability (Pls. 60–63). For later exhibitions he made a number of tall very narrow pots, 24 inches or more in height, which could have come from no other hand. Murray's strength did not lie in his brushwork, which is often insensitive and empty though for the most part well related to the form of the pot. His glazes are admirable in range and quality, as a rule very reserved in colour but occasionally relatively brilliant. In 1940 he left England for Southern Rhodesia, where he died in 1962, separated from his kiln to which he hoped he might one day return.

The most notable of Murray's students was Thomas Samuel HAILE (1909–48), who studied with him for three years at the Royal College of Art and in whose work an echo of Murray's forms may sometimes be traced. But Haile's pots are essentially original and he was by no means to follow any prescribed course. He had a lively exploratory mind not content with studying only the accepted sources of pottery inspiration, and early in his training his imagination was captured by the Surrealist movement and the paintings of Picasso, influences which showed themselves in the decorations on his pots. Writing in *The Listener* of a memorial exhibition of Haile's work held in London in 1951, Patrick Heron claimed that his were 'the first modern pots which bore any relation to contemporary painting' and pointed out that 'ten years and more before Picasso began to design and decorate pots at Vallauris, Haile was creating his essentially contemporary idiom in pot decoration'.

Sam Haile was equally skilled in stoneware and slipware and had a sound knowledge of the techniques of both styles. Much of his later and best work was done in the United States (Pls. 64 and 65), where he went with his wife, Marianne de Trey, also a potter, three years after leaving the Royal College of Art. In the States he explored the American collections, lighting particularly on pre-Columbian sculpture and Pueblo-Indian pottery. He taught and studied at the New York State College of Ceramics at Alfred and later became pottery-instructor in the College of Architecture of the University of Michigan at Ann Arbor. On release from military service Haile began potting in England again, and accepted the post of Clay Industries Adviser to the Rural Industries Bureau. This he combined with his own work, first in Suffolk, at Bulmer's brickyard in Sudbury (Pls. 66 and 67), and later in Leach's former workshop at Shinner's Bridge near Dartington Hall. It was here, just as his work was reaching maturity, that he suffered the fatal motor accident which deprived us of one of the most lively minds in contemporary English pottery.

Henry Fauchon HAMMOND (b. 1914) also began his career as a potter under Staite Murray at the Royal College of Art. Until 1939 Hammond worked chiefly in stoneware, often with successful brush decoration, but his long period of war service was to prove a serious interruption and after demobilisation practical difficulties obliged him for a time to confine himself to slipware, a medium in which he was less at home. Hammond directs the Pottery Department of Farnham (Surrey) School of Art, in which he has the very able collaboration of Paul BARRON (b. 1917), a pupil of Norah Braden. Both Hammond and Barron work in stoneware in such time as their teaching allows and together they have brought their school a reputation for well-grounded and lively teaching (Pls. 68 and 69).

7

LUCIE RIE AND HANS COPER

Both Lucie RIE (b. 1902) and Hans COPER (b. 1920) came to England in the years immediately before the outbreak of the Second World War, Coper from Germany and Lucie Rie from Vienna, where her reputation as a potter was already established. She had also received gold medals in international exhibitions in Brussels, Paris, at the Milan Triennale and elsewhere.

In contrast to English potters of that time whose criteria derived chiefly from early Chinese stoneware or from the English earthenware tradition, Lucie Rie's inspiration was based on the concepts of modern architecture and functionalism current in pre-war Vienna and particularly as expressed in the work of Professor Ernst Plieschke. This architect and designer, with whom Lucie Rie found much in common, was influencing thought in Vienna in ways which paralleled the work of the Bauhaus in Germany, which during pre-war years so profoundly affected the world of design. Earlier in her life Lucie Rie had been deeply attracted by Roman pottery (from Eisenstatt and other sites) in the collection of a relative, where she had been able to handle it at leisure. These were the two mainsprings of her thinking and they permeated her study of pottery at the Kunstgewerbeschule, where Michael Powolny was Professor of Ceramics and where her instruction had also included a course in ceramic chemistry.

When Lucie Rie came to England she brought a few pieces of her pottery with her from Vienna, but English taste at that time appeared hardly sophisticated enough to appreciate the elegant simplicity of her shapes (Pl. 90), and W. B. Honey of the Victoria and Albert Museum made the acute criticism that she was making earthenware pots with stoneware glazes. On some of her pots there were distinctive glazes in a style unjustly dismissed as uncontrolled, in which the bubbling glaze bursts or leaves an undulating 'volcanic' surface (Pl. 91), the antithesis of the smooth closeness of oriental wood-ash glazes for which our potters were striving.

Inevitably it was suggested that Lucie Rie should meet Bernard

45

Leach and although her Viennese work failed to satisfy him entirely he at once recognised a potter of sensitivity and distinction, and invited her to visit him at his pottery in Shinner's Bridge. The experience affected her deeply, particularly Leach's conception of 'completeness' in a pot, comprehending something more than form, body and glaze and extending even to the finish of the unseen part of the foot. For the first time she found herself in the workshop of a potter who was both artist and very experienced craftsman. She saw the attention given to the preparation of clay from local materials, to be followed by the spell-binding, rhythmic kneading of the clay, skills which had been brought from Japan. The visit enlarged her whole conception of making pottery just at a time when her own work and environment had been disrupted by removal from Vienna and when she had hardly begun to use her new workshop in London. And now wartime conditions intervened and she could not resume any serious production until 1945/6.

Lucie Rie began in England by making a little of the reduced earthenware with which she was familiar but soon she was attempting stoneware and porcelain, and for a while made a living by producing ceramic buttons and beads which met a ready sale in the drab conditions of post-war London. For this she employed some assistants, Hans Coper among them. It was a difficult time: she was not only building up her experience in new and more exacting techniques but her meeting with Bernard Leach had been cataclysmic and she was only slowly distilling what she had seen and heard in his workshop. The pots she exhibited in the Berkeley Galleries in 1949, although they held much promise, betrayed some of the uncertainties from which she was suffering. But as she became at home in the slowly reviving city around her, her confidence returned and her native sense of style re-emerged.

At this critical time her association with Hans Coper was of inestimable value. He was able to help her over practical working difficulties; he understood her background of thought and, above all, persuaded her not to be concerned with English stoneware but to return to the inspirations of her work in Vienna. Slowly confidence in her abilities revived and, as George Wingfield Digby has put it, 'she began to recreate her style'. Lucie Rie's exhibition in 1949 had shown mainly the elegant cream raw-glazed porcelain with manganese *sgraffito* bands with which she will always be associated (Pl. 92a). As she extended her technique she began to make substantial stoneware with a thick grey-white glaze, enhancing it with diagonal furrows (Pl. 98). She was also introducing colour, always with characteristic reserve — quiet greens and fine lines or bands of blue or dull red pigment (Pl. 95) and

E. Porcelain Bowl by Lucie Rie. 1953
Uranium glaze with decoration on unglazed manganese band.
Height $3\frac{1}{8}$ inches. Diameter $4\frac{3}{8}$ inches. Mark: LR seal.
The British Council.

later a rich yellow glaze obtained with uranium (Pl. E). She also developed, with Hans Coper, a range of very carefully considered domestic wares: cups and saucers, salad bowls, tea and coffee pots and jugs, all in brown and white. At the same time she returned to the rough geological glazes begun in Vienna, and they became an established characteristic of her work (Pls. 96a and 99).

Exhibitions, frequently shared with Hans Coper, were held in the Berkeley Galleries, and she gained a market in New York with Bonniers, where she held a one-man show in 1954. Her work had from the first received the recognition of architects and she and Hans Coper together were the two potters chosen to exhibit at the Milan Triennale in a group of work sent from England in 1954. There were exhibitions also in Minneapolis, Tokyo and in the Boymans-van Beuningen Museum in Rotterdam in 1960 and again in 1967. In England her understanding of design for present-day living at its most discriminating has brought her a devoted clientèle and a unique place among the potters.

This was given recognition when, in the summer of 1967, the Arts Council arranged a large retrospective exhibition of Lucie Rie's work, only the second time that it has given this distinction to a living potter. In his scholarly introduction to the catalogue George Wingfield Digby defined what is perhaps her most important characteristic when he wrote, 'Here was a studio potter who was not rustic but metropolitan; her work had no nostalgic undertones of folk art', a statement which makes clear a key element in her work not hitherto captured in words. This quality was already discernible (to a degree her later work was scarcely to better) in the exhibition cases showing her earliest pots — some borrowed from Vienna. These confirmed her innate sense of elegance and her ability to be simple without boring, surely the touchstone of distinction. The range of work in the exhibition, both in scale and style, was a revelation even to those who had followed her development. Moreover, it emphasised her growing ability to decorate and complicate the forms of her pots without losing their essential deceptive simplicity, and left no doubt of Lucie Rie's status as a leader among twentieth-century potters.

Hans COPER has already been referred to in relation to Lucie Rie and it seems most probable that without her he might never have given his mind to making pottery. Indeed, it is said that he did so at first with some reluctance. Coper's early training had been as an engineer, but painting and sculpture were always his deepest interests. He came to England in 1939 and almost at once the upheavals and difficulties of war conditions deprived him of any opportunity to develop his considerable abilities.

47

When Hans Coper began to work with Lucie Rie in 1946 he was at first engaged only in helping to make the ceramic buttons and beads with which she was temporarily occupied. Inevitably in the environment of the pottery Coper slowly became involved and began to try his hand on the wheel and think out his own pots. These did not come quickly but gradually an entirely individual style emerged.

Hans Coper has always worked in a restricted range of materials, depending chiefly on his invention of form and confining his use of colour to the full range of browns, from near black to palest buff. In some of his pieces, where the entire surface is the darkest brown, his work comes close to departing from ceramics and has much of the feeling of a bronze (Pls. 107 and 108). Except in some of his early pieces, his pots always have a matt surface on which he works by very personal methods to give subtleties of colour and texture which greatly enhance them (Pls. 110 and 111). Many of Coper's later forms depend on the uniting of two interpenetrating shapes (Pls. 108 and 109), and once he has an idea which he finds satisfactory he usually repeats this, developing and varying it both in size and in surface detail. He has a long-standing interest in contemporary architecture and for a time worked with an architectural development group as consultant on the design of heavy clay products. He is also a member of the Ceramic Department of the Royal College of Art. To an even greater degree than Lucie Rie's, Coper's work shows no evidence of rustic tradition — it belongs completely to mid-twentieth-century thought and environment.

F. SQUARED STONEWARE JAR BY LUCIE RIE. 1967
With incurved lip. Dolomite/limestone glaze.
Body in bands of two differing clays,
one pigmented, giving areas of pale rusty-red
and muted blue.
Height 11 inches. Recessed foot, glazed,
with LR seal in centre.

8

GEOFFREY WHITING, HELEN PINCOMBE, IAN AULD, RUTH DUCKWORTH, EILEEN LEWENSTEIN, JANET LEACH, THE CRAFTSMEN POTTERS' ASSOCIATION, CONCLUSION

There are so many lively and well-established potters working in England today that the choice of subjects for inclusion in the remaining part of this book is bound to be invidious.

In the work of the Midlands potter, Geoffrey WHITING (b. 1919), his initial training as an architect has been allied to a deep-rooted interest in the interaction of earth and fire. In his early childhood Whiting dug clay, coiled it and evolved primitive kilns, and when the war took him to North India he made opportunities for working with village potters, his first and last close contact with vocational potters, though at a primitive level. By the end of his army service pottery had so claimed him that he decided against practice as an architect and, with the help of Leach's *Potter's Book*, set himself to make stoneware. Teaching occupied Whiting briefly in a pottery unit he had been asked to build for Avoncroft College, Bromsgrove, and this he later took over for his own production. In 1955 he moved to larger premises in Hampton Lovett, near Droitwich, where he built a large two-chambered kiln fired with coal and wood. Whiting is especially known for his teapots, in which he has been able to meet all the tricky functional requirements of a teapot and give them a comfortable, well integrated form (Pl. 79). Whiting's stoneware shows the discipline of his architectural training and he believes in using a few simple materials which can be known intimately.

Helen PINCOMBE, born in India in 1908, was educated in Australia. She travelled to England in 1925, came upon pottery in Camberwell School of Art, and continued her study at the Central School of Arts and Crafts. Later she became an exhibitioner at the Royal College of Art, where the outbreak of war disrupted her work. The College had removed to Ambleside, Staite Murray had retired to Rhodesia, and after taking her Diploma Helen Pincombe was asked to join the staff temporarily to teach pottery. While in the Lake District she found herself within reach of Burton-in-Lonsdale (the Black Burton of 18th-century slipware), where the last remaining pottery of eight which were extant in 1914 was making stoneware bottles and kitchen crocks. This contact with a living tradition provided a stimulating addition to her experience, and after the war she set up her own pottery, now in Oxshott, Surrey, quietly developing her stoneware and exhibiting her work both at home and abroad. She is perhaps best known for her bowls and her well-controlled range of high temperature glazes (Pl. 81) and for her concern for standards in the teaching of pottery at all levels.

After service in the Navy during the war, and three years studying painting at the Slade School, Ian AULD (b. 1926) became interested in pottery when training in the Institute of Education, London University. Much of his experience has been gained while teaching, at the Central School in Baghdad (which enabled him to travel in the Middle East and India) and later in the Camberwell School of Art, where Richard Kendall was in charge of the pottery department. Auld has never been at ease with wheel-thrown forms and prefers the limitations imposed by slab-building, the flat surfaces of which he has used for impressed decoration. His interest tends towards ceramic sculpture but he has not abandoned pots with a use, particularly dishes (Plate 80) and pots to hold flowers. In 1965 he became lecturer in ceramics at the Bath Academy of Art and has set up a workshop in the neighbourhood.

It was almost by chance that Eileen LEWENSTEIN (b. 1925) had her first experience with pottery while studying in the Institute of Education, London University. This led her during her last term to read Leach's *Potter's Book* and to decide that she must become a potter. Although for a time committed to teaching, she managed to gain pottery experience in a variety of ways and was associated with the Briglin Pottery. Eileen Lewenstein now works in Hampstead and teaches at Hornsey College of Art. She has worked chiefly in stoneware (Pl. 85), and in recent years a meeting with Catherine Yarrow led her to explore freer methods of using clay and to the making of sculptural constructions. But she has not abandoned the other aspect of her work and has plans for working in porcelain, contrasting free methods of making with this traditionally sophisticated material.

Ruth DUCKWORTH was born in 1919 in Hamburg and came to

England in 1936. She studied painting and sculpture at Liverpool School of Art but attempts to establish herself as a sculptor were unrewarding. Ruth Duckworth's interest in pottery began when she wished to find out how to glaze a piece of sculpture. Having discovered from Lucie Rie that this would involve a good deal more than a glaze recipe, she began to study pottery, first in Hammersmith and later at the Central School of Arts and Crafts. Her training as a sculptor has been evident from the outset and her shapes are often built up by coiling (Pl. 83) or pinching, and recently by other unconventional uses of clay. Her reputation has grown steadily both in England and overseas, and in 1964 she was invited to become artist in residence in the Midway Studio of the University of Chicago, where she remained for two years. This was followed by a commission for a large ceramic mural for the University on which she is at present engaged.

The work of Janet LEACH (b. DARNELL, 1918) bears the impression of her strong personality and she is gaining a leading position among post-war potters. Born in Texas, she studied sculpture, and later pottery, in New York. She met Leach and Hamada at a pottery seminar which they were conducting, and in 1954 travelled to Japan, where she worked with Hamada and spent a rigorous winter in a Japanese country pottery in the mountains. In Hamada's workshop she again met Bernard Leach, and in 1956 came to England and they married. In St. Ives Janet Leach found many responsibilities but she also for the first time had the opportunity to work out her own ideas in pottery. This cannot have been easy in a place with such a strongly prevailing style of its own. Before long she had built a small kiln so that she could experiment with salt glazing, a technique that had not been tried in St. Ives since its early days. She also began to use clay in experimental ways and has made some successful tall cylindrical pots simply formed by wrapping the clay around a base. Her recent work is on a large scale where she seems to feel most at home (Pls. 86 and 89) and there are indications that her significance as a potter is only just emerging.

Michael CASSON (b. 1925) tried his hand at several crafts, particularly woodwork, but, in his own words, he found clay 'more expressive and spontaneous'. Unfortunately the pottery instruction which came his way in training college and school of art proved somewhat negative and his inspiration did not become compulsive until he read Leach's *Potter's Book*. From then on he began to learn by trial and error, at the same time continuing to teach, for which he has a natural gift. Michael Casson has taught pottery to people of every age from 7 to 70. In recent years his work at Harrow School of Art has been particularly successful and as an exhibition in 1966 showed, his students explore an unusually wide range of techniques and at the same time gain a sound understanding of essentials. Since 1959 Michael Casson has been at his Pottery Workshop in Prestwood, Buckinghamshire, where he has developed some excellent stoneware glazes (Pl. 82b), concentrating on their tactile qualities. But it must be said that Casson's contributions to teaching have been to some extent at the expense of his own pots, and he is now limiting himself to advisory work, drawing comfort from the knowledge that Hamada, by his own confession, did not lose his 'tail' till he was over 40 years of age.

In 1958 a group of potters decided to set up a co-operative association 'to sell their work, increase informed opinion and enlarge their own outlook'. They called this *The Craftsmen Potters' Association of Great Britain* and set up their London centre in a small turning off Carnaby Street, where members' work was always on view and could be purchased. The enterprise has been remarkably successful in fulfilling its aims. This has been in no small part due to the practical and diplomatic guidance of the honorary secretary David Cantor and the assistant secretary Pan Henry, both non-potters, who held the group together while it was establishing itself and in 1967 steered its removal to larger premises in Marshall Street, behind Regent Street. Enlargement of the potter's outlook and technical knowledge has certainly been achieved but the record of sales is another indication of the value of the Association, both to the potter and to the general public.

In the fourteen years since the first edition of this book was published, the early Chinese pots have lost some of their first impact on twentieth-century potters, and inspiration now comes from many other sources. Nevertheless, the influence of Bernard Leach is still evident, not only in the proven value of his *Potter's Book* but also because of his capacity for meeting and talking with fellow-potters in a way which encourages and inspires them so that differences of age are forgotten.

The work of many younger potters is moving away from the discipline of wheel-throwing towards other methods of construction — coiling, slab-building and casting — and more experimental uses of clay are being tried. Some of this work crosses the almost indefinable boundary between pottery and sculpture but the essential potter always feels, though perhaps unconsciously, the compulsion to make a shape which can function as a container in however remote a way. Command of technique has made amazing progress in the years since Leach came to St. Ives, infiltrating from the technologists in Stoke-on-Trent and transmitted by working potters from their accumulated experience. Kiln construction and controllable methods of firing, the use of refractories, body-glaze relationship and much else no longer

52

perplex and frustrate. A sound grounding in pottery is available at many schools of art and the emerging potter today scarcely realizes the advantages with which he is equipped. Pottery is also widely taught in general education but it lacks the established standards which music, for instance, enjoys. It is too often regarded as a subject that can be adequately taught after the briefest of short courses, though no one would be engaged to teach a musical instrument on such a basis. Nevertheless, large sums of money are being spent on providing and equipping pottery-rooms in the new schools, though this money is liable to be misapplied. In particular, expensive electric kilns are installed which prevent students from acquiring a realistic understanding of the interaction of fire and clay, experience which could be gained with little outlay in simple kilns which they had constructed themselves. On the other hand more imaginative teaching is spreading, particularly for young children: by the introduction of primitive methods of making and firing they are able to participate with understanding in the entire process, to their great satisfaction.

This slowly accumulating knowledge gives hope for a better informed appreciation of potters' work. Industry, though still for the most part dismissing the individual potter as eccentric and of little account, is liable to borrow some of his more lively ideas, particularly when these stem from contemporary styles of living. The handful of individual potters working in England in the early part of this century are now too numerous to count, and in all parts of the world today there appears a compelling fascination in the clay, the wheel and the mysterious transmutations of firing. Young people are drawn into a career which holds little prospect of affluence and demands dedicated service, a movement which Leach once called the counter-industrial revolution.

In the Far East the potter has always been held in great respect. Today throughout the world he is, for the first time, commanding recognition as an artist in his own right.

The supreme exponent of another art, Pablo Casals, said, in his ninety-first year, 'One must have great mastery to get to the simplest things, the most important thing is sincerity with oneself'.

This above all one would wish for potters today.

53

POTTERS' IMPRESSED SEALS
AND PAINTED MARKS

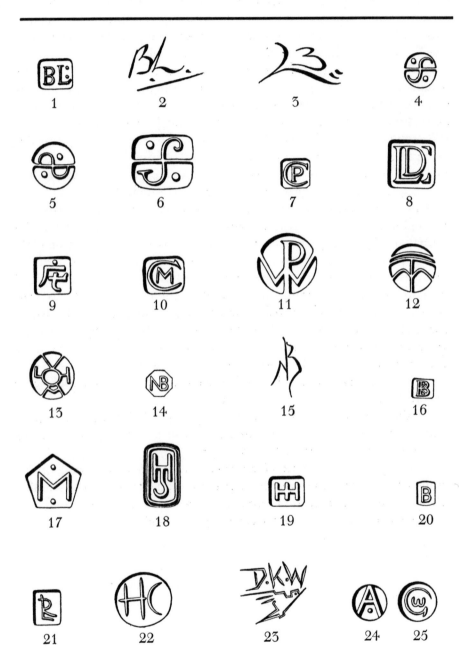

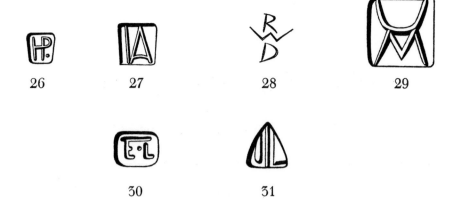

26   27   28   29

30   31

1–3 Bernard Leach; 4–6 St Ives Pottery; 7 Crowan Pottery; 8 David Leach; 9 Shoji Hamada; 10 Michael Cardew; 11 Winchcombe Pottery; 12 Wenford Bridge Pottery; 13 Volta Pottery; 14–15 Norah Braden; 16 Katherine Pleydell Bouverie; 17 W. Staite Murray; 18 T. S. Haile; 19 H. F. Hammond; 20 Paul Barron; 21 Lucie Rie; 22 Hans Coper; 23 Denise Wren; 24 Avoncroft Pottery; 25 Geoffrey Whiting; 26 Helen Pinchcombe; 27 Ian Auld; 28 Ruth Duckworth; 29 Michael Casson; 30 Eileen Lewenstein; 31 Janet Leach.

A SELECTED BIBLIOGRAPHY

Publications in Japan not included

GENERAL

Billington, Dora, *The Art of the Potter*. Illustrated. London, Oxford University Press, 1937

Honey, W. B., *The Art of the Potter*. Illustrated. London, Faber, 1946

Cooper, Ronald G., *The Modern Potter*. Illustrated. London, Tiranti, 1947

Haggar, Reginald, G., *English Country Pottery*. Illustrated. London, Phoenix House, 1950

Leach, Bernard, *A Potter's Portfolio, a selection of fine pots*. Illustrated. London, Lund Humphries, 1951

Digby, George Wingfield, *The Work of the Modern Potter in England*. Illustrated. London, John Murray. 1952

Birks, Tony, *The Art of the Modern Potter*. Illustrated. London, Country Life, 1967

Casson, Michael, *Pottery in Britain Today*. Illustrated. London, Tiranti, 1967

Periodicals

Studio 145, April 1953. Illustrated. *The Crafts then and now*. Leach, Murray, Cardew, Rie, etc. by Peter Floud.

Apollo 62, October 1955. Illustrated. *Cornwall's Studio Potters*. B. Leach, D. Leach, Harry and May Davis, etc. by Denys V. Baker.

Museums Journal 59, September 1959. Illustrated. *Stoneware at York*. Leach, Hamada, etc. by J. A. S. Ingernells.

Studio 159, May and June 1960. *British Potters Today, I and II*. Cardew, Coper, Duckworth, Hammond, Leach, Pincombe, etc., by Henry W. Rothschild.

Pottery and Glass 38.10 November 1960. Illustrated. *Craft and Design*. Rie, Marshall, Duckworth.

56

SELECTED BIBLIOGRAPHY

TECHNICAL

Lunn, Richard, *Pottery, a handbook of practical pottery for art teachers and students*. Illustrated. London, Chapman & Hall, 1903

Doat, Taxile, *Grand Feu Ceramics*. Illustrated. Syracuse, N.Y., Keramic Studio V and VI, 1903/4
Les Ceramiques de Grand Feu. Illustrated. Paris, Art et Decoration XX and XXI, 1906/7

Cox, George, *Pottery for Artists, Craftsmen and Teachers*. Illustrated. New York, Macmillan, 1914

Binns, C. F., *The Potter's Craft, a practical guide*. Illustrated. New York, D. Van Nostrand, 1947

Hetherington, A. L., *Chinese Ceramic Glazes*. London, Cambridge University Press, (2nd Edition), 1948

Wren, Denise and Rosemary, *Pottery Making*. Illustrated. London, Pitman, 1952

Leach, Bernard, *A Potter's Book*. Illustrated. London, Faber (2nd Edition), 1945; Fourteenth impression, 1969.

Cardew, Michael, *Pioneer Pottery*. Illustrated. London, Longmans, 1969

FRENCH POTTERS

Catalogue de L'Exposition D'oeuvres de Céramistes Modernes, 1890–1930. Illustrated. Musée Céramique de Sèvres, 1931

Chavance, René, *La Céramique et la Verrerie*, Illustrated. Paris, L'Art Française depuis Vingt Ans, 1928

Ozonfant, *L'Art de Potier*, Illustrated. Paris, Bonifas, 1930

Valotaire, Marcel, *La Céramique Française Moderne*, Illustrated. Paris, Editions G. Van Oest, 1930

Franklyn, W. *The Master Potter of La Chappelle aux Pots, F. Delaherche*. Illustrated. New York, American Society of the French Legion of Honor, Pamphlet II.6, 1935

ARTIST POTTERS IN ENGLAND

MICHAEL CARDEW

Periodical

Apollo 37, May 1943. Illustrated. *Michael Ambrose Cardew*, Potter of Winchcombe, Gloucestershire, by Ernest Marsh.

THOMAS SAMUEL HAILE

Periodicals

Art News 40, March 1941. U.S.A. *Thomas S. Haile*, London's loss, our gain.

Apollo 44, December 1946, Illustrated. *T. S. Haile*, Potter and painter, by A. C. Sewter.

Architectural Forum 90, March 1949, U.S.A. Illustrated. *Haile*, The Pottery of,

Craft Horizons 2, 1949. U.S.A. Illustrated. *T. S. Haile*, Ceramist.

SHOJI HAMADA

Periodicals

Artwork 5 No. 19, 1929. *Hamada*, Some Modern Potters.

Art Digest 14, January 1940. U.S.A. Illustrated. *Kawai and Hamada*, Japan's two most noted living potters.

Craft Horizons 16, July 1956. U.S.A. Illustrated. *Hamada*, Folk art of Japan.

Studio 144, October 1952. Illustrated. *Leach and Hamada* by D. Lewis.

Craft Horizons 21, November 1961. U.S.A. Illustrated. *Hamada*, The enduring art of, by O. Untracht.

Graphis 18, November 1962. Illustrated. *S. Hamada*, Examples of Contemporary Pottery, by M. Fare.

American Artist 20, February 1964. U.S.A. Illustrated. *Hamada*, a Japanese folk potter.

BERNARD LEACH

Heron, Patrick, *The Changing Forms of Art; Submerged Rhythm, A Potter's Aesthetic*. Illustrated. London, Routledge & Kegan Paul. 1955

Leach, Bernard, *A Potter's Work*, with introduction and biographical note by J. P. Hodin. Illustrated. London, Evelyn, Adams & Mackay, 1967

SELECTED BIBLIOGRAPHY

BERNARD LEACH (*continued*)
Periodicals

Studio 90. November 1925. Illustrated. *Bernard Leach*, The Pottery of, by Michael Cardew.

Atelier I, 101, May 1931. U.S.A. Illustrated. *Leach and Tomimoto*.

Artwork 7 No. 26. 1931. Illustrated. *Bernard Leach*, The Pottery and Tiles of, by John Gould Fletcher.

Apollo 37, January 1943. Illustrated. *Bernard Howell Leach*, Potter, by Ernest Marsh.

Design 48, September 1946. Illustrated. *Bernard Howell Leach*, English Potter, by J. P. Hodin.

Studio 133, March 1947. Illustrated. *Bernard Leach*, Thirty years in the service of ceramic art, by J. P. Hodin.

Royal Society of Arts Journal 96, May 1948. Illustrated. *B. Leach*, Craftsmanship, the contemporary artist potter, by the artist.

Craft Horizons 3, 1950. U.S.A. Illustrated. *The Leach Pottery* at St. Ives, by R. Richman.

Time 55, February 1950. U.S.A. Illustrated. *B. Leach*, Kenzan VII, one of the world's best pottery makers.

Studio 144, October 1952. Illustrated. *Leach and Hamada*, by D. Lewis.

Pottery Quarterly I, 1954. Illustrated. *The Leach Pottery*, Workshop Visit, by Murray Fieldhouse.

Burlington 100, April 1958. *Bernard Leach*, Exhibition of Porcelain and Stoneware in London.

Connoisseur Year Book, 1958. Illustrated. *Bernard Leach*, The Art of, by George Wingfield Digby.

Pottery Quarterly V, 1958. Illustrated. *B. Leach and Hamada*, Exhibitions in London reviewed by Murray Fieldhouse.

New Zealand Potter, 1960. Wellington. Illustrated. *Bernard Leach*, *Essays in appreciation*, edited by Tony Barrow.

Museums Journal 60, January 1961. Illustrated. *Bernard Leach*, Fifty years a potter, with bibliography by G. Wingfield Digby.

Burlington 103, February 1961. *Bernard Leach*, Exhibition at the Arts Council, reviewed by Michael Strauss.

Studio 161, May 1961. Illustrated. *Bernard Leach*, by J. P. Cushion.

Craft Horizons 20, July 1961. U.S.A. *Leach*, East and West by M. C. Richards.

Design 154, October 1961. Illustrated. *B. Leach*, Potter's Philosophy by R. Duckworth.

Pottery Quarterly VII, 1961/2. Illustrated. *Leach*, Fifty years a potter, exhibition at the Arts Council, by Geoffrey Whiting.

Studio International 173, January 1967. Illustrated. *B. Leach*, Exhibition at the Chateau de Ratilly reviewed by J. P. Hodin.

ARTIST POTTERS IN ENGLAND

JANET LEACH

Periodical

Pottery Quarterly IX, 1967. Illustrated. *Janet Darnell Leach*, by J. P. Hodin.

THE MARTIN BROTHERS

Beard, Charles Reilley, *Catalogue of the Nettlefold Collection of Martin ware*. Illustrated, with text. London. Privately printed, 1936

Periodical

Apollo 40, October 1944. Illustrated. *The Martin Brothers*, Studio Potters of London and Southall, Middlesex, by Ernest Marsh.

WILLIAM STAITE MURRAY

Periodicals

Studio 88, December 1924. Illustrated. *W. S. Murray*, Flambé stoneware, by Bernard Rackham.
Apollo 39, April 1944. Illustrated. *W. Staite Murray*, Studio Potter of Bray, Berkshire, by Ernest Marsh.

KATHERINE PLEYDELL BOUVERIE AND NORAH BRADEN

Periodicals

Artwork 6 No. 24, 1930. Illustrated. *N. Braden and K. Pleydell Bouverie*, English Stoneware Pottery by W. A. Thorpe.
Apollo 38. December 1943. Illustrated. *K. Pleydell Bouverie and D. K. N. Braden*, Studio Potters of Coleshill, Wiltshire, by Ernest Marsh.

SELECTED BIBLIOGRAPHY

LUCIE RIE AND HANS COPER

Periodicals

Apollo 59, February 1954. Illustrated. *Lucie Rie*, Potter, by A. C. Sewter.

Architectural Review 116, September 1954. Illustrated. *Hans Coper, Lucie Rie*, Pots in rows, by R. Melville.

Craft Horizons 15, January 1955. U.S.A. Illustrated. *Lucie Rie*, Pottery in porcelain.

Pottery Quarterly III, 1956. Illustrated. *L. Rie and H. Coper*, Exhibition at the Berkeley Galleries.

Design Quarterly 39. 1957. Minneapolis U.S.A. Illustrated. *Lucie Rie*

Architectural Review 124, October 1958. Illustrated. *Hans Coper* and other potters, Stoneware pots at Heals.

Architectural Review 140. October 1966. Illustrated. *Lucie Rie and Dan Arbeid*, Design review, by Ronald Cuddon.

Apollo 86, July 1967. Illustrated. *Lucie Rie*, Exhibition in London, reviewed by J. Burr.

Design 226, October 1967. Illustrated. *Lucie Rie*, Pottery of, by T. Davenport.

INDEX

INDEX

Rackham, Bernard, 24 & note
Rie, Lucie, 45–8, 51, Plates 90–103
Royal College of Art, 22, 23, 37, 43, 44, 48, 50
Royal Institute of Cornwall, Truro, Plate 14
Ruskin Pottery, 20

Seddon, J. P., 18
Sèvres, 15, 16, 22
Shinner's Bridge Pottery, 29, 44, 46
Slade School of Art, 25, 50
Slipware: revival by Leach, 27–8; and by Cardew, 33; use by Leach, 29; by Cardew, 34, 38; by T. S. Haile, by H. F. Hammond, 44
Stoke on Trent College of Technology, 39
Stoke on Trent Museums & Art Gallery, Plate 45

Taylor, W. Howson, 20
Times, The, 29
Tinworth, George, 18
Tobey, Mark, 29
Toft, Thomas, 27
Tomimoto, Kenkichi, 26
Tonks, Henry, 25
Tustin, Sydney, 36

University College of Wales, Aberystwyth, 34
University of Chicago, 51
University of London, Institute of Education, 50
University of Michigan, 44
University of Minnesota, 40

Vallauris, 44
Victoria, H.M. Queen, 19
Victoria & Albert Museum, 25, 37, 45, Plates 31, 44, 56, 59, 62, 67
Vienna, Kunstgewerbeschule, 45
Vumé-Dugame, Ghana, 34, 35
Vyse, Charles, and his wife, 24

Wells, Reginald, 24, 25, Plate 8
Wenford Bridge Pottery, 34–6
Whiting, Geoffrey, 49, Plates 78, 79
Winchcombe Pottery, 33, 34, 36
Wood, Christopher, 43
Worcester Art Museum, Massachusetts, Plate 58
Wren, Denise, 20, Plate 9
Wrotham Pottery, 24

Yanagi, Dr. Soetsu, 26

Ziegler, Jules-Claude, 15

1. STONEWARE JAR BY ERNEST CHAPLET
Thick aubergine to black cuprous glaze suffused with grey;
inside, light turquoise blue
Height 3½ inches. Mark: ⸬ incised. About 1900

Musée National d'Art Moderne, Paris

2. STONEWARE BOWL BY AUGUSTE DELAHERCHE
Dark greenish-blue and light brown flecked glaze
Height 5⅞ inches. Diameter 7⅞ inches
Mark: *Aug Delaherche*, incised. About 1907

Musée des Arts Décoratifs, Paris

3. STONEWARE VASE BY EMILE DECŒUR
Ochrous yellow glaze with areas of light violet
Height 11¾ inches. Mark: *Decœur*, incised. About 1910

Musée des Arts Décoratifs, Paris

4. STONEWARE BOWL BY EMILE DECŒUR
Bronzey green-black glaze over incised decoration
Height $7\frac{7}{8}$ inches. Diameter $13\frac{3}{8}$ inches
Mark: *E. Decœur*, incised. 1932

Musée National d'Art Moderne, Paris

5. STONEWARE JAR BY EMILE LENOBLE
Greenish raw-sienna coloured glaze over incised linear decoration
Height 7 inches. Mark: *EL in a circle,* incised. 1931

Musée National d'Art Moderne, Paris

6. Stoneware Vase by the Martin Brothers
Green-white glaze with rim and inlaid decoration in dark olive green
Body cream. Height $4\frac{1}{4}$ inches.
Mark: *12. 1901. Martin Bros. London and Southall,* incised. 1901

Bethnal Green Museum, London

7. STONEWARE VASE BY THE MARTIN BROTHERS
Cream glaze with irregular inlaid blotches in light tan
Body buff. Height 4¾ inches.
Mark: *3–1907 Martin Bros. London and Southall,* incised. 1907

Victoria and Albert Museum

8. EARTHENWARE VASE BY REGINALD WELLS
Pale grey to white crackled boracic glaze on light red body
Height 8¼ inches
Mark: (Imperfect) SOON *in a frame*, impressed. 1928

Bethnal Green Museum, London

9. Stoneware Jar on Three Feet by Denise Wren
Greenish to red-brown salted ash glaze with shallow incised
decoration. Coarse red body. Height 5½ inches.
Glazed foot with marks: DKW and *Oxshott*, incised. 1960

W. A. Ismay

10. 'RAKU' WARE DISH BY BERNARD LEACH
Red and brown trailed-slip decoration, 'Hare', on cream slip ground
Diameter 13 inches. Made in Abiko, Japan. 1918

National Museum of Folk Craft, Tokyo

11A. 'RAKU' WARE TEAPOT & CUP BY BERNARD LEACH
Dark brown trailed-slip decoration. Sallow-brown glaze
Teapot, height: $3\frac{3}{4}$ inches, diameter: $4\frac{1}{4}$ inches
Cup, height: 2 inches, diameter: 3 inches
Made in Azabu, Tokyo. 1919

National Museum of Folk Craft, Tokyo

11B. 'RAKU' WARE BOX BY BERNARD LEACH
Dull red trailed-slip decoration, with green, on cream slip ground
Diameter: $4\frac{1}{2}$ inches. Made in Japan. 1914

National Museum of Folk Craft, Tokyo

12. Earthenware Jug by Bernard Leach
Covered in dark brown slip. Red body
Height about 9 inches
Made at St. Ives about 1924

13. SQUARE STONEWARE JAR WITH DOMED LID
BY BERNARD LEACH

Moulded. Purplish-black glaze with wax-resist decoration
Red body. Height $6\frac{1}{8}$ inches. Marks: St. Ives and
BL seals. 1924

Muriel Rose

14. LARGE EARTHENWARE DISH BY BERNARD LEACH
'Hills in China with river-bridge'
Light slip ground with dark brown and red slip decoration
under golden-yellow galena glaze. Notched edge.
In centre of foot, rectangular trailed-slip pattern with BL in slip
in centre and date 1929 in border.
Buff body. Diameter: 17½ inches

Royal Institution of Cornwall, Truro

15. LARGE EARTHENWARE DISH BY BERNARD LEACH
Dark brown and red trailed-slip decoration, 'Griffon', under
light golden-brown galena glaze. Underside with bands of trailed-slip.
In centre of foot, rectangular red-slip pattern
with BL in brown-slip in centre and date 1929 in border.
Buff body. Diameter: 18 inches

Mr. & Mrs. George Wingfield Digby

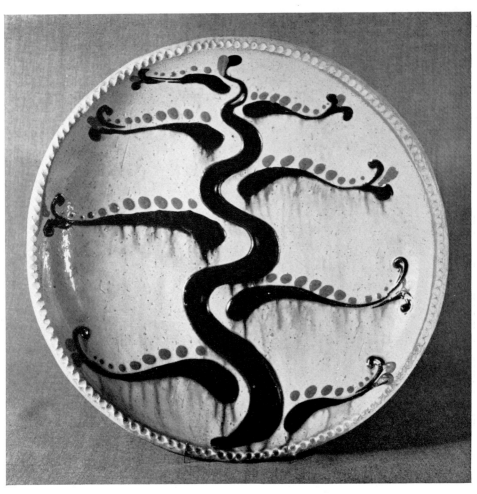

16. EARTHENWARE PLATE BY BERNARD LEACH
Moulded, with notched edge. Creamy-yellow ground (white slip)
with dark brown and red-brown trailed-slip decoration
under galena glaze. Pinkish-cream body.
Diameter: $12\frac{1}{4}$ inches
Mark: Small St. Ives seal. About 1930

Mrs. Bertha Bundy

17. EARTHENWARE PLATE BY BERNARD LEACH
Moulded, with notched edge. Trailed-slip decoration
(white slip on black, with brown in centre) under golden
yellow galena glaze. Light red body. Diameter: 7½ inches
Mark: Square St. Ives seal. About 1934

Bernard Leach

18. STONEWARE BOTTLE BY BERNARD LEACH
Brown-black. Decoration engraved through black slip to buff
body. Height about 11 inches. 1939

19. STONEWARE PLATE BY BERNARD LEACH
Light and dark broken-olive browns. Decoration, 'Pilgrim' in wax
and cut-paper resists. Black slip under light glaze. Light grey body
firing ochre. Diameter: 11 inches. Marks: BL and St. Ives seals, 1951

Shoji Hamada

20. STONEWARE PLATE BY BERNARD LEACH
Light green-grey with olive-brown rim and decoration, 'Birds and
nest', brushwork and sgraffito. Light grey body. Diameter 12 inches
Marks: BL and St. Ives seals. 1951

In Japan

21. STONEWARE JUG BY BERNARD LEACH
Salt-glazed, light buff, notched foot
Height: 6¾ inches. Made in St. Ives. 1961

National Museum of Folk Craft, Japan

22A. PORCELAIN PLATE BY BERNARD LEACH
Over-glaze enamel decoration in red, black and green. White body.
Diameter: approximately 6 inches. Made in Kutani, Japan. 1954

In Japan

22B. PORCELAIN BOX BY BERNARD LEACH
Light bluish ground with incised and painted decoration, 'Bird in
flight' on side. 'Pecking bird' on reverse side. 'Clouds' on lid
White body. Length $2\frac{3}{8}$ inches. Height $1\frac{5}{8}$ inches.
Marks: BL on one end, St. Ives sign on the other, both painted. 1960

Mr. & Mrs. George Wingfield Digby

23A. PORCELAIN POWDER BOX BY BERNARD LEACH
Light bluish ground with bands of darker blue painted over incised
decoration. A frog in brush decoration on lid. White body
Height: 2 inches. Marks: BL incised and St. Ives seal. 1960

Mrs. George Wingfield Digby

23B. PORCELAIN CUP & SAUCER BY BERNARD LEACH
Pale celadon glaze. Cup with spiral flutes. White body
Diameter of saucer $5\frac{5}{8}$ inches.
Marks: BL and St. Ives seals impressed. 1959

Bernard Leach

24. STONEWARE JAR WITH HANDLE BY BERNARD LEACH
Warm white, base and neck dipped in white slip;
embossed decoration on centre front. Cream body, firing red
Height 15 inches. Marks: BL and St. Ives seals. 1945

The British Council

25. STONEWARE JUG BY BERNARD LEACH
Grey-green breaking to olive-brown with red (iron) splashes
Cream body, firing red. Height $10\frac{1}{2}$ inches
Marks: BL and St. Ives seals. 1948

The British Council

26A. PORCELAIN BOX ON THREE FEET BY BERNARD LEACH
Conical lid. Pale celadon glaze. White body. Height 4 inches
Marks: St. Ives seal (3 times) and BL, impressed. 1957

Mr. and Mrs. George Wingfield Digby

26B. PORCELAIN BOWL ON STEM BY BERNARD LEACH
Pale celadon glaze with brown flecks. White body
Height: $4\frac{1}{8}$ inches. Width: $6\frac{1}{2}$ inches. Mark: BL seal inside foot. 1959

Helen Pincombe

27. STONEWARE BOTTLE BY BERNARD LEACH
Warm white with brown flecks, dipped in white slip. Red body
Height: 12 inches. 1956

Anne Marie Fernbach

28. STONEWARE BOTTLE BY SHOJI HAMADA
Rich black *tenmoku* glaze with trailed red (iron) decoration
Light brown body. Height: $6\frac{1}{2}$ inches
Marks: Hamada and St. Ives seals. Made at St. Ives about 1921

City of York Art Gallery – Milner-White Bequest

29A. STONEWARE BOX BY SHOJI HAMADA
Brilliant black *tenmoku* glaze with red brown (iron) decoration on lid
Light sandy body. Height: $2\frac{1}{4}$ inches. No mark. About 1929

City of York Art Gallery – Milner-White Bequest

29B. STONEWARE INK BOTTLE BY SHOJI HAMADA
Black *tenmoku* glaze breaking to red brown
Height: 3 inches. No mark. About 1929

Stoke-on-Trent Museums and Art Gallery – Henry Bergen Bequest

30. STONEWARE BOWL BY SHOJI HAMADA
Light celadon glaze with brown (iron) brush decoration
Whitish porcellaneous body. Height: $5\frac{1}{4}$ inches
No mark. Made at St. Ives about 1930

Gwynneth Lloyd Thomas

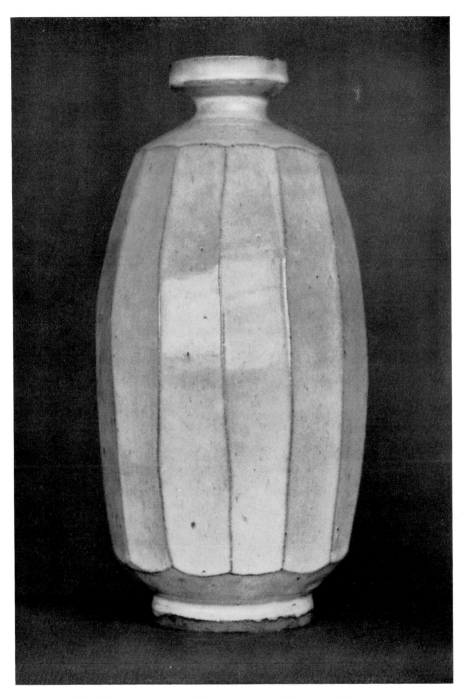

31. STONEWARE BOTTLE BY SHOJI HAMADA
Cut sides. Cream glaze on sandy reddish body. Height $12\frac{3}{4}$ inches
No mark. About 1930

Victoria and Albert Museum

32. STONEWARE TEA BOWL BY SHOJI HAMADA
Thick light-grey glaze on rough body (*tetsou-é*). Reddish sandy body
Height: $4\frac{3}{16}$ inches. No mark. 1940

Mikio Horio

33. STONEWARE TEA BOWL BY SHOJI HAMADA
Cream glaze with light and dark brown (iron) brush decoration
Buff body. Height: about $3\frac{1}{2}$ inches
No mark. 1942

In Japan

34. STONEWARE WINE BOTTLE BY SHOJI HAMADA
Cream-grey glaze with brush decoration in yellow-brown and
black-brown (iron) glaze on glaze. Reddish body
Height: 5 inches. No mark. 1939

National Museum of Folk Craft, Tokyo

35A. PORCELAIN WATER SPRINKLER BY SHOJI HAMADA
Red, yellow and green enamel brush decoration. Grey body
Height: 2½ inches. Length: 3½ inches. No mark. 1941

In Japan

35B. STONEWARE BOWL BY SHOJI HAMADA
Thick light-grey glaze on rough body (*tetsou-é*) with brown brush
decoration. Red-brown body. Diameter about 6 inches. No mark. 1948

In Japan

36. STONEWARE VASE BY SHOJI HAMADA
Cut sides. Greenish-brown (iron) glaze. Red body. Height: $9\frac{1}{2}$ inches
No mark. Spur-marks of small shells on foot. About 1951

57. SQUARED STONEWARE BOTTLE BY SHOJI HAMADA
Cut sides. Sallow-brown (iron) glaze, breaking to yellow
Red body. Height: 11 inches
No mark. Spur-marks of small shells on foot. About 1951.

Christopher Arnold

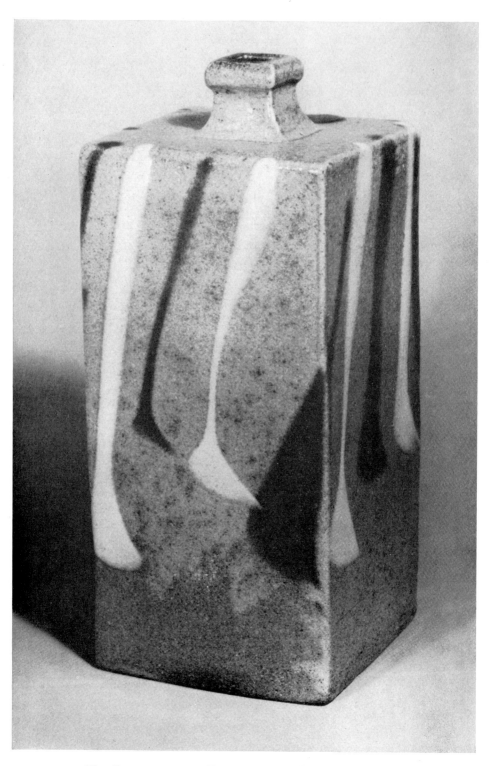

38. STONEWARE BOTTLE BY SHOJI HAMADA
Moulded. Salt-glazed with black and white trailed-slip decoration
Height: 9¼ inches. Width: 3⅞ inches. No mark. 1959

In Japan

39. STONEWARE JAR BY SHOJI HAMADA
Moulded. Black (iron) glaze, upper part with opaque grey-white glaze
Height: $9\frac{7}{8}$ inches. Width: $4\frac{3}{4}$ inches. No mark. 1960

In Japan

40. EARTHENWARE JUG BY MICHAEL CARDEW
Golden yellow to brown. Incised through light slip
with inscription in the Cornish language:
'HEDHEW GWRA GANS SKIANSDA HA DEW VEDN RY
PETH YU DA RAGOSY'
Red body. Height: 6¼ inches. Mark: St. Ives seal. 1924/5

Charlotte Bawden

41. OVAL EARTHENWARE DISH BY MICHAEL CARDEW
Bright golden-brown with yellow trailed slip decoration 'Stag'
Red body. Length: 14½ inches. Mark: Winchcombe Pottery seal. 1928/9

Charlotte Bawden

42. EARTHENWARE JAR BY MICHAEL CARDEW
Golden-brown. Sgraffito decoration through slip. Red body
Height: $17\frac{1}{2}$ inches. Marks: MC and WP seals. 1930

Mrs. Seton White

43. EARTHENWARE CIDER JAR BY MICHAEL CARDEW
Warm brown with golden-brown decoration, trailed slip on dark slip
Red body. Height: 13 inches
Marks: small MC and WP seals. 1936

Robin Tanner

44. EARTHENWARE JAR BY MICHAEL CARDEW
Flecked sallow-brown with light yellow brushed slip decoration
Red body. Height: 14¼ inches
Marks: MC and WP seals twice. About 1937

Victoria and Albert Museum

45. LARGE EARTHENWARE BOWL BY MICHAEL CARDEW
Broken golden brown with light cream trailed-slip decoration
Interior, cream mottled with grey. Red body.
Height: 9 inches. Diameter: 14½ inches.
Marks: MC and WP seals. About 1937

Stoke-on-Trent Museums and Art Gallery – Henry Bergen Bequest

46. Earthenware Jar by Michael Cardew
Greenish yellow brown. Decoration incised through light slip
Red body. Height: 19 inches
Marks: MC and WP seals. About 1937

Michael Cardew

47. EARTHENWARE CIDER JAR BY MICHAEL CARDEW
Black to very dark brown. Decoration incised through raw glaze
Red body. Height: 22 inches
Marks: MC and WP seals. About 1937

Donald Potter

48. EARTHENWARE DISH BY MICHAEL CARDEW
Light yellow with green-black decoration, sgraffito through light
slip to dark slip ground. Red body. Diameter: 9½ inches

Raymond Finch

49. STONEWARE LIDDED BOWL BY MICHAEL CARDEW
Light greenish-grey glaze with sallow brown (iron) brush decoration
Light pinkish body. Height: $5\frac{1}{4}$ inches. Diameter $7\frac{5}{8}$ inches
Marks: MC and Wenford Bridge seals. 1950

The British Council

50. STONEWARE JAR BY MICHAEL CARDEW
Rich bronze-green glaze with brilliant orange-red (iron) brush
decoration, 'Vumé Lily'. Red brown body
Made at Volta Pottery, Vumé, Ghana.
Marks: MC and Volta Pottery seals. 1948

The British Council

51. STONEWARE OIL JAR BY MICHAEL CARDEW
With screw stopper. Black-brown iron glaze with incised decoration,
'Dragon', on upper half. Red-brown body. Height: 30¾ inches.
Made in Nigeria. Marks: MC and Abuja seals impressed on side. 1957

Michael Cardew

52. STONEWARE CASSEROLE BY MICHAEL CARDEW
Three handles, with band of notched ornament below them,
Grey-green glaze with incised pattern through iron
pigment on lid and upper part. Red-brown body
Height: 8½ inches. Width: 10¼ inches
Made at Wenford Bridge about 1957/8

Dr. John Holden

53. STONEWARE SAUCE BOTTLE BY MICHAEL CARDEW
With screw stopper. Dark bronze-green iron glaze with incised
decoration. Red-brown body. Height: 3¾ inches. Made in Nigeria
Marks: MC and Abuja seals impressed. 1958/9

Henry W. Rothschild

54. STONEWARE JAR BY KATHERINE PLEYDELL BOUVERIE
Flecked purplish-brown '*tessha*' glaze. Grey body. Height: 8 inches
Mark: KPB monogram seal. About 1930

Victoria and Albert Museum

55A. STONEWARE BOWL BY KATHERINE PLEYDELL BOUVERIE
Broken grey-green wood-ash glaze with red (iron) splashes
Warm buff body. Height: $2\frac{3}{8}$ inches. Diameter: $3\frac{1}{8}$ inches
Mark: KPB monogram seal. About 1932
University College of Wales, Aberystwyth

55B. STONEWARE BOWL BY KATHERINE PLEYDELL BOUVERIE
Ribbed sides. Green-grey wood-ash glaze breaking to brown on ribs with
red (iron) splashes. Fine red body. Height: $2\frac{3}{4}$ inches. Diameter: 4 inches
Mark: KPB monogram seal. About 1932
University College of Wales, Aberystwyth

56. STONEWARE BOWL BY NORAH BRADEN
Cold-grey flecked wood-ash glaze with red-brown (iron) splashes
Reddish body. Height: $5\frac{3}{4}$ inches. Diameter: 9 inches
No mark. About 1935

Victoria and Albert Museum

57. STONEWARE JAR BY NORAH BRADEN
Green-grey peat-ash glaze with red brown (iron) splashes
Pinkish body. Height: 6½ inches. Diameter 8 inches
About 1939

In the United States

58. STONEWARE JAR BY NORAH BRADEN
Olive-green box-wood ash glaze with red (iron) splashes
Height: 6½ inches. Width: 8⅛ inches
About 1939

Worcester Art Museum, Massachusetts

59. STONEWARE JAR BY NORAH BRADEN
Green-grey to bronze glaze with red-brown (iron) splashes
over transverse ribbing. Yellowish body. Height: 8 inches
Mark: NB, painted. About 1933

Victoria and Albert Museum

60. STONEWARE BOTTLE BY WILLIAM STAITE MURRAY
Cream slip under transparent glaze. Light transverse markings
Pinkish body. Height: 16 inches
Mark: M in pentagon seal. About 1927.

Audrey Debenham

61. STONEWARE JAR BY WILLIAM STAITE MURRAY
Flecked sage-green glaze with red-brown (iron) brush decoration, 'Cattle'
Height: 18¾ inches. Mark: M in pentagon seal. 1928

Fitzwilliam Museum, Cambridge

62. Stoneware Bottle by William Staite Murray
Warm stone-grey crackled glaze over transverse ribbing
Reddish body. Height: $18\frac{1}{2}$ inches
Mark: M in pentagon seal. About 1930

Victoria and Albert Museum

63. STONEWARE JAR 'ANUBIS' BY W. STAITE MURRAY
Buff semi-matt glaze breaking to red-brown over transverse ribbing
Coarse buff body. Height: $19\frac{1}{4}$ inches
Mark: M seal on side and kiln marks under foot. About 1938

W. A. Ismay

64. EARTHENWARE BOWL
'FLORAL GROWTH' BY T. S. HAILE
Brown, strong red and black trailed-slip decoration on cream slip
ground. Red body. Diameter: about 20 inches
Mark: SH joined, in slip. 1940

Dr. W. R. Valentiner

65. EARTHENWARE BOWL
'TRIO' BY T. S. HAILE
Greenish-grey, lightly mottled. Trailed white slip decoration over
black slip, covered with semi-opaque tin glaze
Red body. Diameter: 14 inches. 1942

Eugene Dana

66. EARTHENWARE JUG BY T. S. HAILE
Trailed black, brown and light pinkish slip decoration on
light brown and dipped black slip ground
Light red-brown body. Height: 10 inches
Mark: SH seal. Made at Bulmer's Pottery, Suffolk. 1946

Marianne Haile

67. EARTHENWARE JUG BY T. S. HAILE
Light brown slip with dark brown oval (dipped) slip ornament carrying
trailed and combed light slip decoration. Glazed by partial dipping
Red body. Height: 12¾ inches
Mark: a seal, illegible. Made at Bulmer's Pottery, Suffolk. 1946/7

Victoria and Albert Museum

68A. STONEWARE BOWL BY HENRY HAMMOND
Green-grey glaze with painted decoration, 'Grasses', in cobalt and iron
Buff body firing red. Height: 1¾ inches. Diameter: 3½ inches
Mark: HH monogram seal. 1959.

68B. STONEWARE BOWL BY HENRY HAMMOND
Celadon glaze. Brush decoration in orange-red (iron) covered with
wax resist and *tenmoku* glaze to give greenish-grey.
Red-brown body. Height: about 3½ inches
Marks: HH monogram seal and glaze notes. 1953

Henry Hammond

69. STONEWARE BOTTLE BY PAUL BARRON
Beaten into oval form. Decoration by partial dipping
White ash (*chün*) glaze over dark brown dolerite glaze
Pale sandy body. Height: 6½ inches. Mark: B seal. 1967

Paul Barron

70. EARTHENWARE DISH BY RAYMOND FINCH
Notched edge. Brown trailed-slip on greenish yellow (light slip) ground
Dull red body. Length: $9\frac{1}{2}$ inches
Mark: WP seal. Made in Winchcombe Pottery about 1938

The late Violet Gordon Woodhouse

71. STONEWARE CASSEROLE BY RAYMOND FINCH
Cream glaze, flecked brown, glazed inside.
Light red-brown sandy body. Height: $7\frac{1}{2}$ inches. Capacity: 5 pints
No marks. 1967

Raymond Finch

72. STONEWARE TEAPOT BY DAVID LEACH
Matt-white titanium glaze, slightly flecked, vertical incised decoration
Close light-brown body. Height: $11\frac{1}{2}$ inches overall
Mark: DL seal. 1966

David Leach

73. STONEWARE BOTTLE BY KENNETH QUICK
Silver-grey to pinkish-mauve wood-ash glaze over white slip, with
sgraffito decoration, large flowers on background of horizontal lines
Dark grey speckled body. Height: 11½ inches. KQ and St. Ives seals. 1962

Janet Leach

74. STONEWARE JUG BY WILLIAM MARSHALL
Grey-brown saltglaze with bands of darker brown at lip and base
Impressed diagonal 'Leaf' decoration with pigment over.
Grey body. Height: 5¼ inches. Mark: St. Ives seal. 1956

J. M. W. Crowther

75. Stoneware Jar with Lid by William Marshall
Light greenish-grey flecked glaze under brushed white slip
(*hakemé*) and black and brown brush decoration
Coarse pale body. Height: 4⅜ inches. WM monogram seal. 1966

Muriel Rose

76. SQUARED STONEWARE BOTTLE BY RICHARD BATTERHAM
Dark *tenmoku* glaze below. Cold-grey wood-ash and feldspar glaze above
Speckled reddish body. Height: $9\frac{7}{8}$ inches. No mark. 1966

Muriel Rose

77A. STONEWARE BOX BY RICHARD BATTERHAM
Cut sides, *tenmoku* glaze, flecked on lid
Speckled buff body. Height: 2¾ inches. No mark. 1966

Muriel Rose

77B. STONEWARE DISH BY RICHARD BATTERHAM
Interior glazed olive-green with radial ribbed decoration
Dull red body. Height: 4¼ inches. Diameter: 18¼ inches
Mark: *England* (type impression). 1966

Richard Batterham

78. STONEWARE CIDER BOTTLE BY GEOFFREY WHITING
Grey wood-ash glaze on upper part. Strongly flecked with iron
throughout. Dark red-brown semi-fireclay body.
Height without cork: $9\frac{1}{4}$ inches
Marks: GW and A (Avoncroft Pottery) seals. 1966

Geoffrey Whiting

79. STONEWARE TEAPOT BY GEOFFREY WHITING
Exterior: red-brown *tessha* glaze. Interior: grey-green wood-ash glaze
Yellowish body. Length: 8¼ inches. Height: 4¼ inches
Marks: GW and A seals. 1966

Geoffrey Whiting

80. SQUARE STONEWARE DISH BY IAN AULD
Slab-built. Pale sallow cream glaze darkening to olive. Lightly
incised olive linear decoration on flat rim
Close white body. $8\frac{1}{2}$ inches square. Height: $2\frac{1}{2}$ inches
Mark: IA seal. 1961

W. A. Ismay

81. SQUARED STONEWARE JAR BY HELEN PINCOMBE
Cut sides. Matt dark olive to black glaze breaking to strong iron red
Flecked buff body. Height: $11\frac{5}{8}$ inches
Mark: HP seal in centre of foot. 1964

J. M. W. Crowther

82A. EARTHENWARE BOWL BY MICHAEL CASSON
Slightly squared. White raw-lead and tin glaze. Incised decoration
on two sides. Close red body. Height: $3\frac{1}{2}$ inches
Mark: MC seal on side. 1958

Michael Casson

82B. STONEWARE BOTTLE BY MICHAEL CASSON
Roughly triangular. Matt grey-blue wood-ash glaze, breaking to
olive brown. Close dark-brown body. Height: $4\frac{1}{4}$ inches
Mark: MC incised on foot. About 1960

Muriel Rose

83. STONEWARE BOTTLE BY RUTH DUCKWORTH
Coiled, slightly asymmetrical. Grey brown and blue glaze
poured over matt black vitreous slip, with areas of wax-reserve.
Close grey body. Height: 10 inches. Max. width: $10\frac{1}{2}$ inches
Mark: RWD seal on foot. 1961

W. A. Ismay

84. PORCELAIN BOWL ON STEM BY RUTH DUCKWORTH
Asymmetrical, indented on one side. Pale sea-green to grey glaze
White body. Height: $4\frac{1}{2}$ inches
Mark: RWD. About 1965

85. STONEWARE BEAKER BY EILEEN LEWENSTEIN
Very pale green-grey glaze. Cream body. Height: $4\frac{3}{4}$ inches
No mark. 1963

J. M. W. Crowther

86. SQUARE STONEWARE JAR BY JANET LEACH
Slab built, tapering towards shoulders and circular opening
Grey to grey-black. Decoration in horizontal bands of black slip
on sgraffito pattern (both covered with semi-opaque white glaze)
on dull red unglazed body
Height: 16 inches. Marks: JL and St. Ives seals on side. 1963

Barbara Hepworth

87. STONEWARE JAR BY JANET LEACH
Exterior unglazed with black glaze decoration. Green-grey flecked
glaze inside and on lip. Body: red-brown. Height: 20 inches
Marks: JL and St. Ives seals on side of foot. 1964

J. M. W. Crowther

88. STONEWARE JAR BY JANET LEACH
Squared. Light olive-green glaze with unglazed areas towards
the base showing warm buff body. Vertical impressed markings
Lightly incised lines at neck and shoulder. Height: $14\frac{1}{2}$ inches
Marks JL in triangle and St. Ives seals on side. 1964

J. M. W. Crowther

89. STONEWARE JAR BY JANET LEACH
Brown underglaze with poured semi-opaque white glaze on shoulder
Coarse red-brown body. Height: 14 inches
Marks: JL and St. Ives seals, under glaze. 1965

Janet Leach

90. TERRACOTTA TEAPOT BY LUCIE RIE
Burnished red body. Cane handle. Height without handle: $4\frac{1}{4}$ inches
Mark: LRG over WIEN, painted. Made in Vienna. 1936

Lucie Rie

91. EARTHENWARE JAR WITH LID BY LUCIE RIE
Cream pitted glaze over black slip. Burnished terracotta lid
Red body. Height: $4\frac{1}{2}$ inches. Mark: LRG over WIEN.
Made in Vienna 1936

Lucie Rie

92A. PORCELAIN BOWL BY LUCIE RIE
Cream-white glaze; unglazed brown (manganese) band on inner rim
with incised cross-hatch decoration
White body. Height: $2\frac{1}{4}$ inches. Diameter: $5\frac{1}{2}$ inches.
Mark: LR seal. 1951

City Museum and Art Gallery, Birmingham

92B. PORCELAIN BOWL BY LUCIE RIE
Mirror-black glaze with band of cream on rim inside and out.
White body. Height approx. 3 inches. Diameter approx. 4 inches
Mark: LR seal. 1952

Lucie Rie

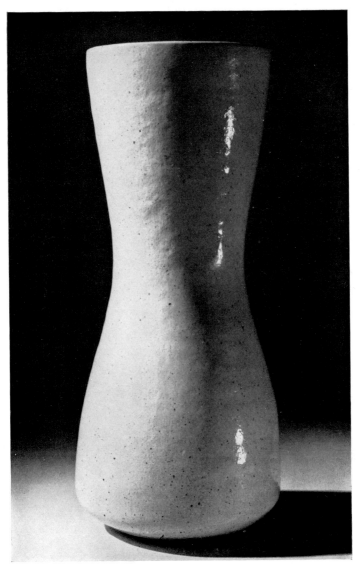

93. STONEWARE VASE BY LUCIE RIE
White glaze slightly flecked. Buff body
Height: 16 inches.
Mark: LR seal. 1952

Lucie Rie

94. ASYMMETRICAL PORCELAIN BOTTLE BY LUCIE RIE
Base of neck compressed to oval
Black-brown with fine diagonal incised decoration showing cream body
Height: $9\frac{7}{8}$ inches. Mark: LR seal. 1960

Museum Boymans–van Beuningen, Rotterdam

95. PORCELAIN BEAKER BY LUCIE RIE
Black-brown with dull red bands near lip and cream unglazed rim to foot
Cream body. Height: $7\frac{3}{8}$ inches. Recessed foot with red ring and
LR seal in centre. 1966

Lucie Rie

96A. STONEWARE BOWL BY LUCIE RIE
Fawn to green strongly pitted glaze showing dark flecked brown body
Height: 3 inches. Diameter at lip: 4½ inches
Mark: LR seal under glaze on foot. 1967

96B. PORCELAIN BOWL BY LUCIE RIE
Exterior: White, with fine black lines of iron pigment inlaid in white
slip, black-brown pigment on foot. Interior: Black-brown manganese
pigment incised with fine lines to show cream body
Diameter: 8¾ inches. Height: 4 inches. 1965

97. STONEWARE BOTTLE BY LUCIE RIE
Pinkish grey. Porcelain clay and limestone slip over coarse body
with copper and manganese additives
Height: 13¼ inches. LR seal on foot. 1966/7

Museum Boymans–van Beuningen, Rotterdam

98. OVAL STONEWARE JAR BY LUCIE RIE
White glaze, flecked with brown and slightly pitted,
over deep diagonal furrows on sides. Dull red body
Height: $7\frac{1}{4}$ inches. Mark LR seal. 1960

Eileen Young

99. CYLINDRICAL STONEWARE VASE BY LUCIE RIE
White heavily pitted glaze on dark grey body with cobalt additive
Height: $4\frac{1}{2}$ inches. Mark: LR seal. 1960

Lucie Rie

100. STONEWARE BOWL BY LUCIE RIE
Mirror-black manganese glaze with minute 'oil spot'
Cream body. Height: about 4 inches
Diameter: about 8 inches. 1965/6

John Sparks Ltd

101. PORCELAIN BOWL BY LUCIE RIE
Covered with white slip with lightly incised lines on exterior
Light grey body. Height: $3\frac{1}{8}$ inches. Diameter: $7\frac{3}{4}$ inches
Recessed foot with LR seal. 1965/6

Mrs. Martin Roberts

102. Porcelain Vase by Lucie Rie
Straw-coloured glaze over porcelain clay and limestone slip with
grey lines (inlaid iron) on lip. Mark: LR seal
Height: 8 inches. 1964/5

Lucie Rie

103. ASYMMETRICAL STONEWARE JAR BY LUCIE RIE
Flattened neck and slightly oval body. Cream semi-matt glaze
with tones of blue-grey and brown flecks.
Dark grey body. Height: $10\frac{7}{8}$ inches
Deeply recessed foot with LR seal underglaze. 1967

Gemeentemuseum, The Hague

104. STONEWARE JAR BY HANS COPER
Unglazed. Linear design incised through dark-brown (manganese)
pigment to cream body. Interior dark-brown
Height: 7½ inches. Mark: HC seal. 1951

The late Phyllis Barron

105. STONEWARE BOWL BY HANS COPER
Unglazed, black-brown, with linear decoration incised through
manganese pigment to show cream-white body
Height: $7\frac{1}{2}$ inches. Mark: HC seal. 1953

Hans Coper

106. STONEWARE BEAKER BY HANS COPER
Black-brown, with linear decoration incised through pigment to
cream body; foot and lower part of pot pigmented but not glazed
Height: $5\frac{3}{4}$ inches. Mark: HC seal. 1952

Arthur Ross

107. STONEWARE BEAKER BY HANS COPER
Manganese black, semi-matt with bands of incised decoration
Dense body firing grey. Height: $4\frac{3}{8}$ inches
Mark: HC seal in centre of pigmented foot. 1962

Lucie Rie

108. STONEWARE VASE BY HANS COPER
Manganese black, semi-matt, lightly incised spiral lines near lip
Dark brown body. Height: $8\frac{1}{4}$ inches
Mark: HC seal on side of foot. 1959

Lucie Rie

109. STONEWARE CUP ON STEM BY HANS COPER
Wide flange at junction of cup and stem. Manganese black,
semi-matt, with lightly incised linear markings
Dense body firing grey. Height: $5\frac{3}{4}$ inches
Mark: HC seal on black foot. 1965

110. STONEWARE VASE ON STEM BY HANS COPER
Upper part flattened oval. Pinkish-cream to grey textured
surface over manganese brown and incised lines
Interior, dark brown. Cream body. Height: 8¾ inches
Mark: HC seal in recessed foot, pigmented. 1966

Muriel Rose

111. STONEWARE VASE ON STEM BY HANS COPER
Upper part flattened oval. Warm cream textured surface over
manganese brown with incised transverse lines. Interior, dark brown
Cream body. Height: $9\frac{1}{4}$ inches
Mark: HC seal in recessed foot, pigmented. 1966

112. STONEWARE BOTTLE BY HANS COPER
Large flanged lip. Manganese brown with cream slip markings over
incised transverse lines. Cream body. Height: $4\frac{1}{8}$ inches
Mark: HC seal on foot. 1966

113. STONEWARE CUP ON STEM BY HANS COPER
Flattened oval with two vertical indentations. Cream textured
surface over dark brown. Interior dark brown
White body. Height: 7¾ inches
Mark: HC seal in recessed foot. 1966

114. TWO ASYMMETRICAL STONEWARE BOTTLES
BY HANS COPER
Cream and buff textured surfaces over dark brown
Interiors, dark brown. Lightly incised linear markings
Cream body. Heights: 10½ and 8 inches
Marks: HC seal in recessed pigmented feet. 1966

115. THREE STONEWARE VASES BY HANS COPER
Funnel-shaped. Buff with pinkish tones and textured surfaces over
dark brown. Interiors, dark brown
Cream body. Heights: $11\frac{1}{8}$, $10\frac{1}{8}$ and $9\frac{1}{4}$ inches.
Marks: HC seal on concave feet. 1966

116. TWO STONEWARE BOTTLES BY HANS COPER
Flanged lips. Cream textured surfaces over dark brown pigment
and lightly incised linear markings
Lips and necks thinly glazed over dark brown slip
Cream body. Heights: 15 and 8½ inches
Marks: HC seal on concave feet, pigmented. 1967

117. ASYMMETRICAL STONEWARE VASE BY HANS COPER
Globular base and flattened oval opening. Buff to cream
textured surface over dark brown pigment. Interior, dark brown
Cream body. Height: 11¾ inches
Mark: HC seal on slightly concave foot. 1967